FAITH,
POLITICS
& PRESS
IN OUR
PERILOUS
TIMES
STEPHEN
BURGARD
EDITOR

Kendall Hunt
publishing company

Cover photo © Mike Nelson/epa/Corbis
Cover design courtesy of Nicholas A. Grassia

Kendall Hunt
publishing company

www.kendallhunt.com
Send all inquiries to:
4050 Westmark Drive
Dubuque, IA 52004-1840

Printed in the United States of America
10 9 8 7 6 5 4 3 2 1

For Beth and Mitch: A couple of uncommon loyalty, courage, and grace.

Contents

Preface

This volume arises from university work I undertook after 26 years on daily deadline as a reporter and editor, the last 12 on the editorial board of the *Los Angeles Times.* When the project began, it wasn't intended necessarily to produce a book. Once it seemed to be a book, it had a different working title, *Covering Religion.* Now at publication time, it has become something more comprehensive: *Faith, Politics, and Press in Our Perilous Times.*

How important is religion that a collection of essays is not only about how to cover it, but also how to understand its place in much of the news? The authors in this collection warn us not to underestimate it as a factor in all manner of events. They do so even as they advise against automatically overstating its significance in individual circumstances. For journalists, religion is a force to be reckoned with unavoidably, even as it intrigues, informs, confounds, and humbles. It poses a challenge at the very core of their purpose, to understand and explain our world.

The project began with several events in the winter and spring of 2008, held on opposite coasts on themes related to religion in the news. I developed the idea as director at Northeastern University's School of Journalism and as a visiting researcher at UC Irvine's Center for the Study of Democracy. Some of these themes have origins in my 1997 book on America's changed religious landscape, *Hallowed Ground* (Plenum), and in the editorials I wrote at the *Los Angeles Times* on religion and politics in the 2000 presidential campaign.

Phil Bennett, now a professor of journalism and public policy at Duke University, was the *Washington Post's* managing editor from 2005 to 2009, and was suggested to me by my Northeastern colleague Walter Robinson, who worked with him earlier at the *Boston Globe.* Phil presided over one of the world's great newsrooms during the War in Iraq and the years following the terrorist attacks of September 11, 2001. In preparing the lecture later adapted for the first chapter, he told me that *the Post's* newsroom had conversations all the time about the press and Islam. It struck me that religion had catapulted beyond the confines of a beat to a place where it was becoming integrated into covering the world and nation.

Phil's talk drew a large turnout on that warm March afternoon in 2008, when the California spring and happenings on a UC campus competed for people's attention. It was apparent that the press's engagement with religion in the modern world was a topic of urgency and interest. His remarks pulled together elements of one of the most important press concerns of our time: how to cover Islam on the global, national, and local stages.

That evening, the Center for the Study of Democracy held a dinner discussion on the 2008 presidential campaign entitled, "Understanding the Religious Voter." That forum, too, provided inspiration for several essays in this volume. Two other participants, Tim Kelly, an evangelical scholar from Fuller Theological Seminary, and Jen'nan Read, a professor at Duke University, are represented.

The next month, a second forum was held on my home campus at Northeastern in Boston. This time the focus was journalism education. Participants in the morning session are contributors to this project as well: Debra Mason, executive director, Religion Newswriters Association & Foundation and director, Center on Religion & the Professions, University of Missouri; Ben Hubbard, chair emeritus of comparative religion at Cal State Fullerton; and Munir Shaikh, who attended with his colleague Shabbir Mansuri of the Institute on Religion & Civic Values. Ben deserves special mention for his advisory role in my transition from the newsroom to the academy, and for his unfailing friendship and wisdom through every stage of this project. Shabbir has been a friend and supporter of my work for a long time.

From the two-coast forums it was on to the idea of a book collection, to include some other participants. We have added distinguished writers, all my current or former colleagues either in journalism or from the university. I am most grateful for their efforts on behalf of journalism education: Rami Khouri, a fellow at Harvard's Belfer Center, and director of American University of Beirut's public policy institute; Jack Miles, the Pulitzer-Prize winner for *God: A Biography* and a distinguished professor at UC Irvine; Bill Lobdell, a former *Los Angeles Times* religion writer; Alan Schroeder of the Northeastern School of Journalism.

Northeastern students past and present have made a considerable contribution. Megan McKee has written a chapter built on her undergraduate research that I hope inspires other students. Two graduate students were assistants at various stages: Yerina Ranjit and James Gachau, and thanks to our grad coordinator, Belle Adler, for making this possible. James has suggested some of the questions at the end of chapters for student discussion. Nick Grassia, a graduate student in the design course of my colleague Gladys McKie, has done the cover.

I also want to acknowledge a number of other special individuals who made this book possible.

Three directors of the Center for the Study of Democracy were unwavering in their enthusiasm for incorporating press and religion into the center's work: Russ Dalton, the center's founding director; Willie Schonfeld, a former dean of UC Irvine's School of Social Sciences; and the current center director, Bernie Grofman, who lent the center's co-sponsorship to this project.

At Northeastern, Bruce Ronkin, interim dean of the College of Arts and Sciences, graciously allowed research time for the writing and editing. His predecessor, Jim Stellar, gave early support, and once joked that *Hallowed Ground* was the only book written by an incoming faculty member he actually read cover to cover. I also value the priority the School of Journalism's faculty places on our department's research and writing; at a retreat each fall, we take time for a short salon where we hear about each other's work.

Larry Thomas, one of California's most astute political observers, was instrumental in facilitating my connection with the UCI research center through his role on its leadership council. My sister, Elizabeth Dater, and her husband, Mitch Jennings, provided encouragement throughout, and I dedicate this book to these two wonderful people.

This project has drawn from a realization that understanding religion is not separate from the practices and good habits of regular news gathering. My former *Los Angeles Times* colleague Jack Miles suggests that reporters don't need to be oracles to ask the right questions or to imagine what might be the consequences of the policies they cover. They just have to make use of information that is there for them already, and then show up prepared for assignment. One hope is that this book helps journalists avoid being surprised by things that may have gone unaccounted for by policymakers and opinion leaders, but that they should know.

The time also seems right for a collection of essays that carries the conversation begun in 2008 to a broader audience of students and writers in journalism, communication studies, religious studies, political science, and international affairs. We live in an interdisciplinary age, and religion and journalism lend themselves well to those connections. I hope that this book will be informative and useful for anyone interested in the important crossroads of journalism, faith, and politics.

Stephen Burgard
Boston, 2010

Introduction

A RELIGIOUS PEOPLE AND THE PRESS TODAY

Stephen Burgard

Since September 11, 2001, the news media in the United States have been compelled to make sense of personal faith, politics, and the power of religious institutions and movements. Religion is challenging journalists on a range of complex topics that include Islamic fundamentalism, the religious dimension of presidential campaigns, and the clergy sex abuse scandal.

The role of the press as democracy's mediator is critical to understand the news at home and abroad. The growth of the religious element has occurred at the same time that journalism itself has been in a period of upheaval, with the burst of online voices and the restructuring of long-time media giants because of the economic and digital transformation of the field. This edited volume, containing essays by leading journalists, scholars, and Pulitzer Prize winners, aims to contribute to an understanding of the intersection of faith, politics, and press in this complex period.

For years, religion coverage was an afterthought. Then editors and reporters got religion, creating beats and special sections. Broadcast outlets did some good work, but not a significant amount. Today, the arena for religion reporting has changed. Generalists, not just specialists, need to know what's going on. There has been little to prepare either group for the complexities of the 21st century; little to make them savvy about resources on the web; and little to brace them for the new economic reality of job reductions in the journalism work force that often leave generalists to know something about everything.

As budgets have shrunk, resources in news organizations are being reallocated. Moreover, in the new world, we need reporters, editors, and producers who know that religion is not necessarily something separate from the secular news. It actually may be driving big events. Our hope is that today's journalists will be able to draw on the perspectives in this volume to help them understand changing times.

Similarly, it no longer is possible for current or future journalists to think of understanding religion as something apart from their regular education, training, or qualifications to cover the day's news. Courses that introduce students to journalism and communications, and also those that address international relations, political science, and religion, may be wise to consider the confluence of faith, politics, and policy.

In some ways, this critical need also provides an answer for the doubters about the value of journalism education who turn up periodically at Poynter Online's Romenesko website.[1] Journalists today cannot possibly know everything. However, considering the importance of religion in the news, there is little excuse for them to come to the story unprepared. That education goes beyond learning conventional and digital skill sets. In our complex world, it also must include developing a base of knowledge and cultivating life-long learning habits that go with the curiosity that journalists must have.

We know that journalists, especially in these times, are trying to make sense of deep and complicated news developments. In a post for the website Getreligion.org, Terry Mattingly, a religion columnist for Scripps Howard News Service, lamented the pressure religion reporting was under because of drastic cuts at news organizations. He noted, "The problem, of course, is that there is more religion news out there than ever, not less, and the beat is getting more complex, not less." [2]

Mattingly suggested the need for a more informed group of generalist reporters and editors, and offered thoughts on the challenges ahead. He took note of non-profit and denominational sources, as well as information from groups like Planned Parenthood and Focus on the Family. But he questioned whether these groups could be trusted to cover themselves objectively.

He concluded that the future would consist of having good websites for niche audiences that supplemented the traditional work of wire services and national newspapers. "I certainly am not prepared to schedule a funeral Mass for the religion beat or for religion news. I would not be doing the jobs that I do if I felt that way," he wrote.[3]

With the help of experts, this book explores these and other aspects of that future. Few if any texts on basic journalism or introduction to news (as opposed to practical lab courses in news writing) provide significant attention to the religious dimension. Given the prevalence of religion in the news, this book is intended both for introductory courses on the news landscape and for more advanced journalism students and practicing journalists wishing to know more about how religion shapes events.

The religious dimension can spring suddenly in the news, even when the focus is squarely on national or political stories. One example came in the summer of 2009 at the funeral and burial of Sen. Edward M. Kennedy of Massachusetts. In the homily, the priest who had ministered to Kennedy in his final days on Cape Cod identified the spiritual bearings of a political leader whose career was secular, and whose chronicled personal problems had obscured any consideration of a person of faith. The Rev. Mark

Hession connected the politician with the man of private conviction, identifying the Biblical foundation for Kennedy's advocacy for those on the margins.[4]

Prof. Benjamin J. Hubbard, a contributor to this volume, later commented to me in an e-mail exchange: ". . . It is the 'faith' element that reporters shy away from, perhaps because they are unable to sort out the moral core from what they perceive as pious or sectarian material that has no place in secular reporting. "

Religious considerations have a way of surfacing even in the regular news reports. In the spring of 2008 as the presidential election year unfolded, all the major presidential candidates had some religious connection that arguably could help the electorate make more informed choices about what made them tick. These included a questionable relationship with a minister, a Methodist faith to inform a candidate's life-long view of political engagement, relations with religious conservatives, and other things. Dramatic changes in our makeup as a people, and the attention given to faith and values in politics have contributed to an already complex political dynamic. Not long after Sen. Kennedy's death, as the Congress debated health care, his son Patrick got in a flap with his bishop in Rhode Island over his position on abortion. Religious concerns about federal funds for abortion again came up in the important special election to fill Sen. Kennedy's vacant seat. Here was religion rising again, this time over national policy.

Finally, we have the currents that can spring up in breaking news, such as the horrific shootings at Fort Hood, Texas, in the fall of 2009, which raised anew concerns about militant Islamic fundamentalism. These examples provide even more evidence for Mattingly's conclusion that there is a lot of religion news to be reported.

This book aims to provide some of the best available guidance on integrating religion coverage into mainstream news writing and editorial decisionmaking. Preferably, this sensibility should be developed early in a journalism student's learning experience. This book arises from a premise that this should be part of a reporter, editor, producer, or blogger's learning curve. It also is intended to be a resource for future religion specialists, and for people going into international affairs, politics, and religion and philosophy.

The book is divided into three sections: religion and the news in the post-September 11 world; religion in the 21st century with attention to new technology and specialty reporting; and covering the new religious landscape.

The first chapter assesses the challenge of covering Islam on the world, regional, and global stages in the post-September 11 world. Phil Bennett, a former managing editor of the *Washington Post* and now a professor at Duke University, writes that the press has been faced with an entirely new set of mandates in a changed world, and that learning about one of the world's great faiths challenged an entire newsroom. This happened at every level of coverage, from global to regional to neighborhood block. Developing this kind of awareness will be a task for all who will come in the press in the next generation.

Rami Khouri, an international journalist and scholar, addresses religion and nationalism in the world's trouble spots. Accurate reporting of foreign news arises from the proper understanding of different forces in the emerging world. Some of the points of contention are truly religious and some are not. It is important for journalists to sort out the sources of conflict, and explain them to readers, viewers, and listeners. This chapter is designed to explain the difference between religious fundamentalism and the powerful forces of nationalism by drawing on the experiences of the Mideast conflict.

Understanding the nature of religious and ethnic conflict is addressed in the third chapter. Jack Miles, the Pulitzer prize winning author of *God: A Biography,* and editor of a new collection on world religions, uses Iraq as a case study to assess what journalists and policymakers need to know to understand conflicts that arise from religious and ethnic quarrels. Drawing on specific regional examples, this chapter explores the difficulties for policymakers and the press in making sense of religious conflict on the global stage.

Prof. Hubbard, chair emeritus of comparative religion at California State University, Fullerton, has written widely on religion and media, and previously edited a standard collection from the first generation of religion writers. His essay traces the evolution of the religion beat and charts its growing significance in today's changing world. His essay reprises some of the memorable religion-in-politics moments of recent decades, and places them in a context to help explain our own times. The 2008 presidential campaign demonstrated the urgency of understanding religious elements in politics, and the author reviews the significance of these developments.

In the second part, we look at how religion coverage itself has been changing: new tools, advanced and specialized reporting, and new outlets for young reporters to consider.

One important challenge for journalists will be how to find out information when there is so much to know about religion. Today, in addition to complicated world events and a dynamic social and religious landscape in America, we also have new social attitudes and patterns of thinking. For instance, in the summer of 2009, the Pew Research Center released a new look at the decades-old concept of a "generation gap," wherein younger people were found less inclined to think that religion was very important, and to have attitudes that were more fluid and tolerant on such cultural issues as gay marriage and interracial relationships.[5] Such trends challenge even the expert religion beat reporters, and pose daunting obstacles to reporters, editors, and producers who encounter religious elements in their work, perhaps for the first time.

Debra Mason, head of Religion/Newswriters, and director of the Center on Religion & the Professions at the Univ. of Missouri, guides future reporters and editors through the new world of online resources. One of them, her organization's "ReligionStylebook," came in handy as the guide for establishing uniformity in the many religious references from different contributors to this book.[6]

Prof. Mason's organization provides other guidance for religion reporters, including such teaching innovations as web-based tutorials. She sums up some of the traditional methods of developing the religion beat, and argues that the landscape for the 21st century has changed completely with the availability of new materials on the web. These resources make possible a new depth of understanding for the public, and reporting for regular religion reporters. It provides a front row seat in covering material that previously may have seemed arcane.

Bill Lobdell, a former *Los Angeles Times* reporter, was witness to some of the biggest stories in journalism in recent years as a religion writer. Along the way, he exposed serious questions about the operations and finances of some TV evangelists, and explored some of the devastation wrought by the Roman Catholic Church's sex abuse scandal. He wrote about his journey in his 2009 book, *Losing My Religion* (Collins). His chapter, excerpted from the book, recounts a part of that reporting, and along the way, provides insights into the task of the religion writer working at longer length. Thus, our hope is that the volume will go beyond an introduction to religion reporting and also take the reader to an appreciation of advanced work.

Journalists who are experts on certain kinds of other stories at times encounter religion as it enters their specialty. Prof. Alan Schroeder, of Northeastern University's School of Journalism, is a leading authority and author on presidential debates. In his chapter, he explores the unconventional forum held in the summer of 2008 at Saddleback Church in Lake Forest, CA, where Pastor Rick Warren hosted the presidential candidates Barack Obama and John McCain in a forum that had some but not all of the characteristics of a presidential debate.

From there we go to an example of student work, and what it might suggest about possibilities for future practitioners in the emerging world of citizen journalism and blogs. Much has been written about the potential for news, analysis, and commentary on changing platforms. One of the many things now clear is that new journalism forms will allow expanded coverage of topics that may have been limited by space or time considerations in newspapers, television, or radio. That suggests that reporters covering issues where complex social policy is tinged with religious considerations may have outlets to do more explanatory journalism in the future. Who better to experiment in this area than a student very much like those who will read this book?

The question considered by Megan McKee was, how do you cover a back story of an important public debate between media-savvy partisans on an issue like gay marriage? Massachusetts became the first state to allow it, but the mainstream coverage was concerned with the aftermath of a court case, the legislative maneuvering that followed, and the positions of the advocates pro and con. Megan went where other reporters did not, tracking down authors of letters to the editor in Boston area newspapers, to explore their thinking. These were thoughtful faith-based citizens not included in mainstream media discussions of the court decision, the legislative debate, or the public conflict between gay activists and anti-gay rights forces. This kind of student journalism has implications for citizen journalism, where more detailed reporting and perspectives on religion are now possible. As students write for websites that cover communities around universities, this can supplement traditional religion reporting.

Finally, in the third part, we look at the new religious landscape and how to understand it.

It is easy to overlook the nation's moral and religious center, which now is made up not only of traditional mainline church folks and other people who consider themselves spiritual, but also immigrants whose religion informs their political concerns. In Chapter 9, I explore the current implications of trends in religious diversity I first wrote about in 1997 in *Hallowed Ground* (Plenum). This essay reflects on our recent politics and national experience, and how the press, if it is too preoccupied with extremists, can miss the influence of faith on politics and policy among independents and moderates. To understand the country, reporters and editors need to take the time to understand the religious center.

The next two chapters explore the social and religious infrastructure of this new diversity and invite journalists to think broadly about the religious population. Jen'nan Read, a Carnegie scholar based at Duke and formerly at UC Irvine, has studied the diversity of the new Islamic population. There are surprising findings that can help the public and journalists understand an important dimension of the domestic story in the age of ideological conflict between western values and religious perspectives.

The theme of understanding a faith-based population extends to religious conservatives in the fundamentalist and evangelical traditions. Prof. Tim Kelly, until recently director of the DePree Public Policy Institute at Fuller Theological Seminary in Pasadena, CA, looks inside the minds and hearts of modern evangelicals. He explains how they can be different from the conventional Christian right.

The image of the fire-and-brimstone evangelical often arises in media reports on powerful figures such as Pat Robertson. It is an accurate portrayal of only a narrow band of media-savvy leaders. The evangelical movement is more complicated, and easily escapes nuanced understanding by the press. In explaining the concept of principled centrism, Prof. Kelly describes why the evangelical population is far more diverse and pragmatic than typically portrayed in political reporting. To report well on religious conservatives, it is important to understand how they think.

How should journalists approach learning about faith groups they may be unfamiliar with? In the last chapter, Munir Shaikh of the Institute on Religion and Civic Values explores what reporters ought to be asking. His organization, formerly the Council on Islamic Education, has years of experience working with book publishers and educators to eliminate stereotyping about Islam. The council developed standards for evaluating such things as basic understanding of a religious tradition, fairness, accuracy, and knowledge of terms. These time-tested principles can be extended to help reporters understand any unfamiliar faith-based perspective, not just Islam.

Taken together, the chapters in this book portray a new reportorial arena where religious factors are never far removed from events. Taking these considerations into account will add depth, nuance, and accuracy to the news report, worthy goals for any reporter, editor, producer, or blogger.

ENDNOTES

1. Poynter Online, Romenesko: http://www.poynter.org/column.asp?id=45.
2. RIP the religion beat? (update), Terry Mattingly, Getreligion.org, Aug. 27, 2008.
3. Ibid.
4. "Senator Kennedy's Funeral: The Homily Part 2," YouTube.com.
5. "Study finds widening generation gap in U.S.," Hope Yen, Associated Press, June 29, 2009. The full report, "Social and Demographic Trends: Pew Research Center" is available at pewsocialtrends.org.
6. "ReligionStylebook," at "ReligionWriters.com: Resources, tools and training for writing about religion" http://www.religionwriters.com/.

PART 1

Religion Reporting in the Post–September 11 World

CHAPTER 1

The Challenge of Covering Islam

Phil Bennett

This chapter is adapted from a chancellor's lecture the author delivered at UC Irvine under the auspices of the Center for the Study of Democracy on March 3, 2008. He was managing editor of the Washington Post *at the time, and since has become the Eugene C. Patterson Professor of the Practice of Journalism and Public Policy at Duke University.*

When I was managing editor of the *Washington Post,* I was drawn into a debate over whether the newspaper's stylebook, which spells out the rules of grammar and usage in the paper and online, should adopt the word "Islamist." This might seem a pretty trivial question in the scheme of things. But words matter—they should matter particularly to journalists, and words like Islamist matter in a particular way: they are labels. They help define the identity of a person, a group, a country, or an idea.

In this case, some editors on *the Post* foreign desk, including two who have spent years covering the Middle East, argued that Islamist was the most accurate term to describe a political movement that bases itself on Islamic law. It's a more specific term than Islamic, which describes anything having to do with Islam. Islamist, they say, will help readers distinguish between Hamas, for example, and the Red Crescent Society.

But there were dissenters to this view. Among them was Sabaa Tahir, a copy editor on the foreign desk. Sabaa is a native of California, a graduate of UCLA, and a Muslim. She said that Islamist was too broad a term to be meaningful. In our internal debate, she wrote to her colleagues that Islamist movements "can be extremist or moderate, pacifist or belligerent, anti-western, anti-Sunni, anti-Shiite, anti-Sufi, anti-women, anti-Israeli, anti-Russian. I worry that if we start using it, over time, we'll cease to explain it properly."

In making her case to me, she said that the purpose of journalism is to confront and explore the world's complexity. If that takes a few more words, then we should use them.

In the end, we decided to approve the use of "Islamist," but to warn reporters and editors from using this or other labels as substitutes for more precise descriptions. The deeper discussion that this modest debate reflected continues, however, and it touches on two important questions of identity. The first involves the historic and monumental process to determine the nature and roles of Islam, a faith practiced by 1.3 billion people in virtually every country on the planet. The second involves the mission of the U.S. press coverage of Islam, one of the largest and most important challenges facing American journalism.

I approach the subject of the press and Islam with humility, and even some anxiety. This is as broad a subject as I can imagine. And it excites intense passions and disputes. There is a fierce battle to categorize and dismiss anyone who steps into the public square to advance a perspective on these matters. So, I'll offer one more piece of labeling information: about me. I am not a scholar or practitioner of Islam. I am also not a pundit, opinion writer, or talk radio host. I'm a journalist. As an editor, I made decisions about what we cover and how we cover it. I've been responsible for the fairness, accuracy, and depth of our coverage. I've tried to be guided by the facts, and to absorb different points of view. If I have a conscious bias, it leans toward a belief in stories and storytelling. As managing editor, it was my job to ensure that our stories were as close to the truth as is possible, given the limitations of our medium—and of ourselves.

I believe the natural position of a journalist is to be an outsider. In my experience, the best journalists inhabit the border between what's inside and what's outside of a situation, roaming across the space that joins and separates the parties to a conflict. I believe this is as good a vantage point as any for observing, reporting on, and understanding what is occurring within Islam, and in the relationship between Islam and the West.

This is not to say that I think the U.S. news media as a whole have embraced this opportunity. Quite the contrary. At a critical time, they have failed to produce sustained coverage of Islam to challenge the easy assumptions, gross generalizations, or untested rhetoric that shape perceptions of Muslims. There continues to be a shortage of two main staples of quality journalism: long-term, probing investigations and immersion journalism, on the one hand; and, on the other, well-informed, nuanced reporting in the routine daily stories that make up most of what we call "the news."

Some Good Coverage

And yet I see several important and, I think, transformative signs of progress. At some news organizations, among some journalists, exceptional coverage of Islam and of Muslim communities has created new models for others to follow. Some of these accomplishments are signs of how far there is still to go. But they point in the right direction. I am going to describe in a moment what I think is working. First, I want to take stock simply of the extraordinary volume (in both senses of the word) of reporting about Islam. Every day, stories are published in newspapers and magazines large and small that add to an ongoing narrative. Choosing just from some recent magazine covers, I could cite these:

- A piece in *The Economist,* examining whether Islam and democracy are compatible, asks, "Can rule by the people be reconciled with the sovereignty of Allah?"

- *Foreign Policy* magazine sports a cover that imagines: "A World Without Islam."

- The cover story in an issue of *Islamica* magazine proclaims: "Media Wars."

- The *New York Times Book Review,* with an ominous gauzy cover, organizes an entire issue around the single word: "Islam."

- The cover of the international edition of *Time,* under a headline freighted with stereotypical assumptions, presents evidence of "Europe's Muslim Success Story."

I could cite dozens upon dozens of other pieces. And I would not have to go deeply into the archives to draw up extensive coverage, for example, of the contentious debate about Muslim activism on one campus that reflects America's diversity today — UC Irvine.

Despite all the attention, this coverage leaves many readers unsatisfied. Criticism comes from all sides. Some complain that it is too soft. Others that it is too hard. Many complain that it is incomplete. *Islamica* put it this way: "Today, despite almost daily coverage of Muslims and the Middle East, English-language media broadcasts and publications consistently fail to demonstrate a critical understanding of the region's history, culture and context."

Some critics blame inadequate coverage for perpetuating a negative and crude image of Islam among non-Muslims. An ABC-Washington Post poll in 2006 showed that 46 percent of Americans have an unfavorable view of Islam, double what the percentage was in early 2002. People's views became more favorable the more familiar they were with Islam. But six out of ten Americans confessed to lacking a basic understanding of the religion.

Statistics, Studies, and Data

There is a wealth of statistics, studies, and other data available to alleviate this ignorance, or color, between the bold lines of our basic knowledge. Even among those of us who consider ourselves fairly well informed, some of these figures challenge what we think we know. Let me list just a few about American Muslims:

- There are between 2.3 million to six or seven million Muslims living in the United States. Nobody knows for certain because the Census does not ask about religious affiliation.

- A nationwide survey in 2007 by the Pew Research Center captured the diversity of American Muslims. About two-thirds were born outside the United States, immigrating from 68 different countries.[1]

- Although in American popular culture a Muslim is likely to be portrayed as an Arab, only slightly more than one-third of foreign-born Muslims in the United States are from Arab countries. Almost one-third are from South Asia. The third largest source of Muslim immigrants is Europe.[2]

- African-Americans make up between 20–40 percent of Muslims in this country.[3]

The Pew survey found that Muslim-Americans are largely assimilated, happy with their lives, and hold moderate views of many of the issues that divide Muslims and non-Muslims around the world. The study found that Christians and Muslims attend religious services in similar percentages (45 and 40). It found that fewer Muslims than Christians said that religious institutions should express political or social views.

The Pew study described a generation gap in which younger Muslims in the United States are more likely to express a strong sense of religious identity. They are more likely to describe themselves as pious. Younger Muslims in this country are also more likely than their parents to say that suicide bombings in defense of Islam can be sometimes justified.

Overall, 75 percent of American Muslims say they are concerned about the rise of Islamic extremism around the world. But they are very skeptical that the U.S. war on terror is effective or even a sincere effort to reduce terrorism.

Aggressive law enforcement since 2001 resulted in 510 people being charged in the United States with terrorism-related crimes through 2006, according to New York University's Center of Law and Security.[4] About 80 have been convicted, mostly for providing material support to groups designated as terrorist organizations. Three people with ties to Islamic extremists have been convicted of planning or attempting a terrorist act in the United States. Only Richard Reid, the "shoe bomber" who tried to blow up a transatlantic flight, has been convicted of carrying out an attempt.

While immigration of Muslims to the United States declined in the aftermath of September 11, 2001, it has surged back. In 2005, more people from Muslim countries became legal permanent U.S. residents — nearly 96,000 — than in any year in the previous two decades.[5]

The Framing of Conflict

Everything I have just mentioned has been in a newspaper story. Why aren't these pieces of the puzzle known more widely? The answer partly has to do with the framing of the conflict between Islam and the West after the attacks of September 11 and the U.S. invasions of Afghanistan and Iraq. For most of the period after the attacks, the best journalism on this subject has fought against the tide of public perception. It has also overcome reduced resources in most newsrooms. Accomplishing this has required courage and ingenuity not only from individual journalists but also from news organizations.

On September 11, there were only a handful of American journalists capable of writing about Islam with any fluency. An even smaller number knew anything about al-Qaeda. On the day of the attacks, no American television network had a bureau in a predominantly Muslim country anywhere in the world. Newspapers were better positioned — *the Post,* for example, had bureaus in Cairo, Istanbul, Jakarta, and Jerusalem — but I think it's fair to say that our knowledge of Islam's political, spiritual, and cultural dimensions was not as intimate or authoritative as the moment demanded.

The lack of knowledge and experience in the press invited oversimplification. This phenomenon was influenced also by the trauma of the attacks and the forceful response of the Bush administration. An exotic and threatening new lexicon entered public discourse devoid of important context: jihad, madrassa, Sharia, hijab, Wahhabi.[6] And not just words; photographs and video clips, cloned from the same shallow pool of understanding, were presented over and over until they lost even the ability to startle. Irreconcilable portraits of Islam — the Islam of peace and the Islam of terror — became the halves of an equation that didn't add up.

For years, few U.S. newspapers or television stations had paid attention to local Muslim communities. In the immediate aftermath of the attacks, these communities turned further inward. Mosques were vandalized, businesses searched, individuals harassed. Under a program called "Special Registration," overseen by the Department of Homeland Security, about 83,000 immigrant men from Muslim countries were fingerprinted, questioned, and photographed. More than 13,000 were placed in deportation hearings. None was charged with terrorism.

Many American Muslims felt under siege, an expression one still hears frequently. This did not put many in the mood to field inquiries from the press. When Andrea Elliott of the *New York Times* was assigned to write about Muslims in the New York area, she encountered one closed door after another. Half-joking, she came to refer to her job as "the-no-one-will-talk-to-me-beat."

Elliott kept knocking on doors, however, and eventually gained the trust of Sheik Reda, the imam of a prominent Brooklyn mosque. She spent six months reporting a series that revealed a world of surprises about the social, political, and spiritual challenges faced by the imam in post-September-11 New York. The series was awarded a 2007 Pulitzer Prize.

So much of the power of good journalism is the power of surprise. As I read and re-read dozens of stories about Islam, and spoke with the authors and subjects of some of them, one thing that surprised me was how much humor was in them. Maybe my surprise was a reflection of how solemn or grim I expected the stories to be. But I think it's telling in other ways.

Sheik Reda, the immigrant imam portrayed in the *New York Times,* laughed while telling the story of a recent immigrant in his mosque. In an effort to adapt to her new country, she dialed 911 to inform the New York City police of her suspicion that a relative back in Cairo was stealing her inheritance. I read elsewhere, in another story, about the television producer launching the hit Canadian sitcom "Little Mosque on the Prairie." In the *Washington Post,* the British writer Safraz Manzoor wrote a fiery manifesto for the Outlook section called, "It's Time for Muslim Comedians to Stand Up."

Good Journalism and Truth-Telling

And then there are the countless wry proverbs and sayings from Muslims that journalists catch in their nets from Rabat to Baghdad to Jakarta. The *Washington Post* correspondent Anthony Shadid, who claims there is no funnier city in the world than Cairo, sent me this ecumenical one: "The donkey who carries Jesus on his back to Jerusalem still comes back a donkey."

I mention this theme because humor is one path to complex truths. As we all know, there is often something behind it, sometimes something darker. Sheik Reda, so adept at breaking the ice with an amusing anecdote, collapsed from the exhaustion of ministering to his Brooklyn community under surveillance, distrust, and the pressures of assimilation. The Canadian sitcom struggled at first to find Muslim actors for its cast. The Outlook piece on Muslim stand-up was greeted with a smattering of applause, but also a cascade of hate mail.

The often ironic or self-deprecating proverbs of many Muslims in the Middle East are sometimes born of resignation, humiliation, or hatred. Another supplied by Anthony Shadid, heard often in Iraq, says, "Since we're already in hell, why not one step further?"

These bittersweet and paradoxical insights remind me that good journalism cannot be measured by comparing the number of positive stories versus the number of negative stories, as some critics of the press insist. The accuracy and value of journalism is measured not by whether it delivers good news or bad news, but by how close it brings you to the truth.

Many models of the best U.S. journalism on Islam are long-term projects by our leading newspapers and magazines. This was the case with Andrea Elliott, Paul Barrett of the *Wall Street Journal,* Hanah Allam of McClatchey Newspapers, and Anthony Shadid.

But what about the more routine daily stories, especially those appearing in mid-sized newspapers and on local television where most Americans get their news? I watched two of these stories unfold recently that seem worth reflecting on.

Coming Soon: The 'Mecca of America'

In the summer of 2007, the town of Walkersville, Maryland, home to about 6,000 people and an hour's drive from the nation's capital, was informed that a real estate developer intended to sell 244 acres of farmland to the Ahmadiyya Muslim Community USA. The Ahmadiyya, who worship at a mosque in suburban Washington, planned to build a retreat center, gymnasium, and several homes for its membership. The land—which, interestingly enough, goes by the Biblical name Nicodemus Farm—would also host the sect's annual festival, drawing 5,000–10,000 visitors to the gently sloping fields off Route 194.

The reaction of townsfolk to news of the impending sale was swift and vehement. Over six months, more than 20 hours of hearings before the zoning board were held in a packed Town Hall. Thousands of pages of public comments were recorded. A group calling itself Citizens for Walkersville was formed and launched the inevitable website. One member said the Ahmadiyya would transform Walkersville into "the Mecca of America." The president of the citizens' group wrote: "Through a behavior-authorizing verse of the Koran, the Muslim concept of 'deceive the infidel' can and will be used against us! You are the infidel! Folks, this is not the Walt Disney generation of the early 1960s where it was a small world after all. The ulterior motives by encroachers cannot be simply dismissed as harmless and diversifying. We must look at world geopolitical circumstances."

For their part, the Ahmadiyya launched an ambitious campaign of public diplomacy. They hosted an open house for Walkersville residents. They gave interviews and took out newspaper ads. Over ten weekends, members of the mosque went door to door trying to explain their history, their views, and the peaceful purpose of their project.

This was big local news. It attracted coverage from Canada and in the *International Herald Tribune,* and *the Post* wrote two straightforward news stories in the Metro section. But mostly it was a story for the local papers, *The Gazette* and the *Frederick News-Post.* All told more than 150 stories, letters, and columns were published about the unfolding drama.

At first, the clash of civilizations narrative played well. Newspaper stories described Walkersville as an isolated hamlet, where the mayor ran the feed store and hosted a weekly dominoes game. Townsfolk protested they were not intolerant, just conservative, though many stories conveyed a veiled suggestion of redneckism.

The Ahmadiyya were portrayed with general sympathy, but shallowly. Not a single story went into depth about the group, which since its founding a century ago in Pakistan has a history of persecution within Islam as a heretical sect. Who were they? What did they believe? Why did they choose Walkersville? It was noted without irony that one spokesman for the group, a 60-year-old pharmacist named Intisar Abassi, lives next door in Frederick, where he works on biowarfare vaccines at the Army's Fort Detrick.

As the case dragged on, the tactics of opponents shifted—and so did the tone of news coverage. Instead of "world geopolitical circumstances," critics focused on traffic, water, sewage, and sprawl. Some months later, citing these concerns, the zoning board rejected the sale and sent the Ahmadiyya packing. The decision was supported by editorials in the *Frederick News Post.*

The project director for the Ahmadiyya, Syed Ahmad, who in his day job is a senior economist for the Federal Housing Finance Board, told me after the decision: "At the beginning it was all about Islam. And in the end it was all about traffic. They realized that they were going to lose if they talked about religion because the media was going to beat up on them. Talk about traffic and the media becomes your friend."

When I drove through Walkersville for the first time, none of the press coverage had prepared me for the look of the place. Yes, there is a timeworn main street. Yes, the Nicodemus Farm is an impressive hunk of land. But Walkersville is hardly a backwoods antique. Downtown Frederick, the largest city in this part of Maryland, is 15 minutes away. A Protestant megachurch, The Calvary Assembly of God, is within walking distance; its Easter Musical attracts some 2,500 worshippers each year. Even the president of the Citizens for Walkersville doesn't live in Walkersville, but in a nice, new development in suburban Frederick.

So, here you had a lot of encroachers competing for a place in Walkersville's future. Among them, the Ahmadiyya might have been the least openly afraid of assimilation. This is a story I wish I'd read.

Syed Ahmad told me that in the end he had come up with what he called the five percent theory. Night after night, he said, the same 300 people showed up to oppose the sale, out of 6,000 Walkersville residents. They represented the extreme, in his view. They controlled the debate, he said, and the outcome.

'An American Who Believes in Islam'

Around the same time as Walkersville was having its Muslim experience, another, even more public controversy was unfolding next door to Washington, DC in the Commonwealth of Virginia. This one also resisted easy answers.

In 2007, the governor of Virginia appointed Dr. Esam Omeish to serve on a new statewide immigration commission. Dr. Omeish is the chief of general surgery at a Fairfax, Virginia, hospital. A graduate of Georgetown University, he moved to the United States as a teenager from Libya. In his early 40s, he is a charismatic speaker, well-connected politically, easygoing with the press.

Omeish is also president of the Muslim American Society, an organization accused on various websites of links to terrorism because of the group's roots with the Muslim Brotherhood. He is on the board of the Dar Al Hijrah Islamic Center, which was investigated after the September 11 attacks because two of the hijackers had befriended the iman and briefly attended the center.

Shortly after Omeish's appointment to the immigration commission, a state legislator called attention to a video made in 2000, and posted on YouTube, in which Omeish extolled the virtues of "jihad." Omeish resigned from the commission under pressure. He said he was the victim of a smear campaign and partisan propaganda, and a misunderstanding of the term "jihad."

I met him one day after the controversy had faded for lunch in a strip mall in suburban northern Virginia. He had come from the operating theater, and he made me a gift of the Quran. Omeish is a highly engaging person. He has lectured about Islam to U.S. military officers at the National Defense University, and said he meets regularly with the F.B.I. to improve the bureau's relations with local Muslims. With a smile, he calls himself a "fundamentalist, in a good sense."

Omeish told me he thought press coverage of his resignation, and more broadly of the Islamic center, was basically fair, but incomplete. He said: "Islam is portrayed as incompatible with American values but the absolute opposite of that is true—and that compatibility is not present in the press. Islam is a mechanism for Americanization. Can we inculcate our Muslim values into the mosaic of America? That would be our contribution."

He told me it would be "nonsense" to apply Islamic law in the United States, or to support the Muslim Brotherhood. "This is not Egypt!" he said. "I am not a Muslim who is living in America. I am an American who believes in Islam."

In the debate about who is a moderate Muslim and who is an extremist, what does it mean to be a "fundamentalist, in a good sense?" Would Dr. Omeish fit into a version of Syed Ahmad's five percent theory? Or is he a leader of a Muslim American majority that will reconcile differences of faith and secular society to change what it means both to be Muslim and to be American?

I suppose the answer to these questions has to do with the character of a person's beliefs. This is very tricky terrain for journalism—and one that cries out for original and probing exploration. Before saying goodbye to Dr. Omeish I asked him why other Muslims had not spoken out about the Walkersville's case. Was it because they view the Ahmadiyya as apostates? He looked at me quizzically, and paused. "If you ask me about the Ahmadiyya, they are not Muslims," he said. "But at the end of the day they can do what they want. If I were on the city council of Walkersville I'd approve it!"

Islam is a global phenomenon, and a global story. Most reporting in the United States about Islam comes from foreign correspondents based overseas. This coverage is dominated by political and military conflict, either among Muslims, between Israel and Hezbollah and Hamas, or between Islamic groups or states and the West, particularly the United States. Islam is at the center of what officials in Washington call "the long war."

For all sides, the media are what military planners call part of the battle space. Osama bin Laden, Ayman Zawahiri, al-Qaeda in Iraq, and others all use broadcast media and the Internet to get out their message. Michael Leiter, the acting director of the National Counterterrorism Center, was quoted in *the Post* saying that a conflict of ideas was a "key center of gravity" in the battle against al-Qaeda and related groups. He said that terrorists "aggressively employ messages related to current events, leverage mass media technologies and use the Internet to engage in a communications war against all who oppose their oppressive and murderous vision." He added, "We must engage them on this front with equal vehemence."[7]

In recent years, coverage of Islam overseas has improved greatly in depth and sophistication. The times have required it. The election of Hamas in 2006 gave a deeper Islamic character to a brutal conflict between Israel and the Palestinians. The Israel-Lebanon fighting of 2006 cast new attention on Hezbollah. The election of President Ahmedenejad sharpened conflict with Iran. Changes of government in Indonesia and Turkey gave an opportunity to explore the fault lines between religion and secular states. Pakistan and Afghanistan are at the top of the news.

Gone are the days when foreign correspondents stuffed Bernard Lewis or Edward Said in their bags as they ran to the airport. Today, journalists have greater first-hand experience of the major issues from the top down and from the irreplaceable access to the richness and immediacy of daily life.

Coverage of Iraq has been pivotal in this development. This was not something we might have expected. The U.S. invasion in 2003 was not explicitly about Islam. Its purpose was to topple a secular dictator and presumably release the democratic longings of Iraqis to create a modern state compatible with American interests and values. But something else happened. Instead, the fall of Saddam Hussein caused a Shiite awakening, conflict, and then a Sunni awakening.

At the time of the invasion, I was the foreign editor at *the Post*. Our correspondent in Baghdad during the invasion was Anthony Shadid. As I edited Anthony's dispatches each night, I was amazed by how often the word "God" appeared in his stories in the voices of Iraqis. Not just "God willing," but "Please God, help us. God save us. Only God will solve our problems. If God writes that you'll live, you'll live. If God writes that you'll die, you'll die."[8]

In the midst of the shock and awe, Anthony wrote a story about a mother taking her son, a soldier, to the bus station in Baghdad as he was being mobilized for the front to fight the Americans. The article contained this exchange: "'There is no god but God,' Karima told Ali at their parting, uttering the first phrase of the shahada, the central creed of Islam. As he bought a 30-cent ticket and boarded a red bus, Ali completed the couplet. 'Muhammad is the messenger of God,' he said."

This was not traditional war reporting. Anthony's attentiveness to the role of religion made him the first American journalist to appreciate the importance of Moqtada Sadr and Ali Sistani; figures barely recognized by the architects of the invasion. Recalling that period in Iraq, Anthony later wrote: "I thought religion basically drove the reporting back in 2003 and 2004. In some ways, it was sad. Religion became the mechanism for redefining identity, often in parochial and intolerant ways. But it allowed us to convey a sometimes very visceral context for the ways Iraqis were making sense of the world around them."

Work like Shadid's created a new standard for depth of reporting about Islam in the U.S. press, not just as a political force, but as a cultural, social, spiritual presence in the lives of millions of people.

The Iraq war also led to the rise of a new generation of Arab-American reporters. Shadid won the 2004 Pulitzer Prize for his coverage of Iraq. Leila Fadel of the McClatchey Newspapers Baghdad bureau won the prestigious George Polk award in 2008. Nancy Youssef and Hannah Allam, also both of McClatchey, and Ashraf Khalil of the *Los Angeles Times* have done distinguished work.

Coverage of Iraq has carried a terrible price. The war is by far the most expensive story in the history of the *Washington Post*. Its cost in human terms has been far greater. Thirty-two journalists and 12 support staff were killed in 2007, bringing the total number of media personnel killed between 2003 and March of 2008 to 174. Among those killed was *Washington Post* reporter Saleh Saif Aldin, an Iraqi, who was shot to death in the fall of 2007 while on assignment in Baghdad. By early 2008, almost one-third of all reporters at the *Washington Post* had worked in Iraq. This experience was carried back into our newsrooms and informed our local, national, and international coverage.

Especially since the murder of *Wall Street Journal* reporter Daniel Pearl, first-hand reporting on terrorist groups remained a very limited field. We largely were unable to explore in-depth questions about the relationship between religious belief and political violence. Is religious fervor the cause or effect of political violence? What are the roles of political, cultural, or tribal influences in molding violent groups killing and dying in the name of Islam? In "the long war," these are strategic questions.

The Media Landscape

I have been asked whether Islamic societies are inherently hostile to a free press. In the Arab world, restrictions on journalists aim at suppressing criticism of the state or challenges to its authority. Today, the fashion in many countries is away from overt acts of violence or imprisonment of journalists towards less blunt instruments of control, such as lawsuits, regulations, and restrictive licensing. On February 12, 2008 all but two of the 22 countries of the Arab League voted to impose new restrictions on satellite television broadcasters. The rules required stations "not to offend the leaders or national and religious symbols" of Arab countries. Article 6 of the draft required satellite TV stations "to refrain from broadcasting anything that would harm God, religions, prophets, messengers, sects and religious figures of all sects."

It is notable that the news of these regulations was splashed across the screens of one their main targets, the Qatar-based station Al Jazeera. The booming success of Al Jazeera, and of other stations such as Al Arabiya, has shown the huge demand by a pan-Arab audience for more varied news, more open opinion and freer debate. Jazeera is far from ideal. But it has pushed boundaries.

Not surprisingly, majority Muslim countries with more dynamic political systems tend to have a more robust and independent press. The Indonesian press is one of the freest in Southeast Asia. In Turkey, tensions continue between hard-line nationalists and the press. But President Abdullah Gul, of the Islamic-oriented Justice and Development Party, launched constitutional reforms to change laws governing freedom of expression.

In the Islamic Republic of Pakistan, the news media fought back against censorship, intimidation, and violence to become, according to polling, the most trusted institution in the country. Despite former President Musharraf's crackdown on independent broadcasters in 2007, the press has played a central role in holding the government accountable and, in the eyes of some analysts, the country together.

Self-criticism is a hallmark of a free society, and a function of a free press. Firas Ahmad is the young deputy editor of *Islamica* who wrote the editorial I quoted earlier about the Western news media's failure to present a complete picture of the Muslim world. When I spoke with him, he also blamed the attitudes of some Muslims toward the press. He said, "Seventy-five percent of my criticism falls on Muslims who don't understand if you don't want to be demonized that communicating your story today requires accepting an independent media and how it tells your story. Propaganda never changes anyone's mind."

Shahed Amanullah, the editor of altmuslim.com, echoed this point in a post addressing Muslim media. He wrote: "The value of an independent Muslim media is greater than simply being a more effective PR machine. These voices are needed to ask tough questions and spur critical thinking within Muslim communities, and take us beyond the defensiveness, dismissiveness, whitewashing, and self-promotion that we have become so used to in our internal dialogue. Muslims in the West are savvy and voracious consumers of the Western media. So, why then should the Muslim media be afraid to rise to that same level of professionalism and open inquiry?"[9]

One way for Muslims to have greater influence on the mainstream news media — and on society at large — is for more to work in newsrooms. As Firas Ahmad of *Islamica* wrote: "If Muslims do not want to suffer the indignation of political irrelevance for many elections to come, instead of giving money to politicians, they should start investing in journalism scholarships."[10]

A few years ago, Shabina Khatri, then a reporter at the *Detroit Free Press,* started the Muslim-American Journalists Association. Shabina grew up in Michigan and was managing editor of the newspaper at the University of Michigan. She was involved in a number of efforts to educate her non-Muslim colleagues about Islam. At *The Free Press,* she organized a "fastathon" for non-Muslims during Ramadan and encouraged forums where journalists could ask questions about the faith.

She told me that while younger Muslim-Americans follow the news intensely, the number entering journalism remains small. Her organization has a little more than 100 members. At the *Washington Post,* where more than 700 journalists work in our newsroom, my Muslim colleagues say there are not more than 8 or 10 Muslims. That strikes me as a low number.

I've heard different reasons for this: American Muslims remain suspicious of the media. Talented would-be journalists prefer to work for Muslim publications. Immigrant parents steer their children away from professions like ours where job security is weakening and starting salaries are low.

The debates inside Muslim communities and the changing media landscape make this an extraordinarily dynamic period. New ways of communicating news and information are taking shape as new actors emerge with stories to tell and a need to be well informed. Some of this discussion takes place in specialized websites or niche publications where like-minded people feel comforted by having their own views confirmed. But there are exciting alternatives emerging.

Important new spaces are opening up in the mainstream media for storytelling and direct participation that didn't exist a few years ago. And there is an audience for them. When *the Post's* innovative online site, *On Faith,* organized a weeklong project entitled, "Muslims Speak Out," the essays, commentary, and live discussions drew 700,000 page views.

At *The Post,* I wanted more Muslim readers, but also more Muslim journalists. I wanted to see deeper coverage of young Muslims coming to terms with their faith in present-day America. I wanted more stories about issues facing African-American Muslims. Muslims in America occupy the intersection of major currents of our society: race, religion, immigration, national security, and politics.

Overseas, the U.S. press has shown that we can get beyond the stereotypes and easy markers of Islam's role in the world. We need to bore into the serious questions of terrorism and the networks and organizations behind it. We also need to give our readers genuine and authentic access to the diversity and breadth of the Muslim experience, which is unfolding on a global scale.

My view is that Muslims in the United States are in a process of moving from being "them" to being "us." Journalism plays a role in transforming "others" into us. This is not necessarily a happy story; it does not mean papering over conflicts or uncomfortable truths. It does mean crossing boundaries—sometimes on a map, sometimes in your head—to engage honestly with how we are all influencing each other's lives. This journey is already underway. It's a story I want to read. It's a story that we should be telling.

SUGGESTED DISCUSSION QUESTIONS

1. How would you assess the *Washington Post's* coverage of Islam in the period after the terrorist attacks of September 11, 2001?

2. What do you make of continued criticism of general reporting on this subject even with the examples of excellence cited by the author?

3. What shortcomings does he cite and what are your own observations as a consumer of news?

4. Is the criticism of the press in this area consistent with complaints you read or hear in other kinds of news coverage, or is this something different?

5. In the author's opinion, how should journalists cover Islam and its impact in the world?

6. Why are all the facts presented in this chapter about Muslims in America not well known?

7. How have more probing and more open media organizations and journalists played a role in opening up the Muslim world?

8. How can independent Muslim media help the Muslim world be better viewed?

9. How can journalism transform Muslims in the United States from being "them" to being "us"?

ENDNOTES

1. The Pew Research Center for the People and the Press, "Muslim Americans: Middle Class and Mostly Mainstream; War on Terror Concerns," http://people-press.org/report/329/, May 22, 2007.

2. *Ibid.*

3. *Ibid.*

4. Terrorist Trial Report Card: U.S. Edition, http://www.lawandsecurity.org/publications/TTRCComplete.pdf.

5. http://en.wikipedia.org/wiki/Immigration_to_the_United_States.

6. Editor's note: Journalists and students wanting definitions of these and other terms can see "ReligionStylebook" at ReligionWriters.com, http://www.religionwriters.com/tools-resources/religionstylebook.

7. Statement for the Record of Michael Leiter, Director (Acting), the National Counterterrorism Center Before the Senate Select Committee on Intelligence's, http:www.ntc.gov/press_room/press_releases/2008-0533.pdf, May 6, 2008.

8. Anthony Shadid, *Night Draws Near: Iraq's People in the Shadow of America's War*, Henry Holt and Company, 2006, p. 175.

9. Shahed Amanullah, "Western Muslims need a 'fourth estate'," http://www.altmuslim.com/a/a/a/2466/, April 9, 2007.

10. Firas Ahmad, "Our Obama problem," http://www.altmuslim.com/a/a/a/2676/, February 20, 2008.

CHAPTER 2

Religion and Nationalism in International Conflict

Rami G. Khouri

The author is a Palestinian-Jordanian and U.S. citizen whose family resides in Beirut, Amman, and Nazareth. He is director of the Issam Fares Institute for Public Policy and International Affairs at the American University of Beirut. His journalistic work includes writing books and an internationally syndicated column, and he also is editor-at-large of the Beirut-based Daily Star newspaper. He has edited newspapers in Lebanon and Jordan, reported for the Washington Post *and* Financial Times *from Amman and the region, and was a Nieman Fellow at Harvard. He comments regularly for the BBC, NPR, CNN, and others. He also is a senior fellow at Harvard's Belfer Center in the Kennedy School of Government.*

Understandably, the Western media have increased vastly their coverage of events and trends in predominantly Islamic societies in the Arab-Asian region since September 11, 2001, given the importance of dealing with terrorism. Unfortunately, with few exceptions, they have echoed and amplified the failure of most politicians and public figures, which is to confuse critical forces at play in many Islamic societies. These forces are mainly nationalism, religion, identity, terrorism, politics, and resistance. Each on its own is a major dynamic; together they comprise a force that redefines entire societies.

In cases such as Iran, Hezbollah, Hamas, or al-Qaeda, the impact ripples beyond the Arab-Asian region to touch power centers in Washington, London, and Moscow. These forces largely have been ignored or misinterpreted by the prevailing analyses in Western power centers. The parallel poor quality media coverage of these phenomena has only disseminated the analytical and political weaknesses of small groups of political and security officials to the wider public. The consequences have been striking, and unfortunate. They are also avoidable, and correctable.

The following are most important: (1) The role and impact of religion in Islamic societies have been vastly exaggerated and misinterpreted, often creating a misplaced over-emphasis on religious causes of people's behavior when in fact it is actually the result of other motivations. (2) The combination of the trauma of the September 11 terror attack and the religious rhetoric of Osama Bin Laden, al-Qaeda, and related terror groups has distorted Western perceptions of any group that uses religious rhetoric, causing an unfortunate prevalent association between political violence and the Islamic religion. (3) Many in the West have been blinded by the reality that Islam has served Muslims in the same way that Christianity, Judaism, and Buddhism have served men and women of those faiths across time. Individuals, groups, or entire societies tend to turn to religious values, promises, and rhetoric as effective mobilizing forces to address political or socio-economic grievances. (4) Terrorism and political violence are widely seen in the West as local problems in Islamic societies, reflecting either religious or political extremism, without seeing the wider regional and global web of policies and actions that have sparked the emergence of these criminal phenomena. Specifically, the genesis of terror groups largely neglects the important impact of the policies of Arab-Asian autocratic regimes, socio-economic stress, Israeli occupations of Arab lands, and the invasions and presence of American, British, and other foreign armies. The research of Prof. Robert Pape at the University of Chicago on motivations for suicide bombers, in particular, confirms the overwhelming prevalence of the desire to liberate one's land from foreign military occupation as the prevalent motive.[1]

The persistence of terror movements that often speak in the rhetoric of Islam is a growing threat to those Islamic societies first and foremost, and also to other countries in the Middle East, Asia, Europe, and North America where terror attacks have occurred on an irregular basis since the early 1990s. The key to dealing successfully with this threat is a multi-faceted approach, and requires going well beyond religion as the primary dimension of analysis. It requires that we accurately understand: (a) the nature and aims of cult-like terror movements that attract relatively small numbers of followers; (b) the many different manifestations of Islamic sentiment throughout society, in political, social, economic, religious, and nationalist forms; (c) the significant differences among al-Qaeda-like global organizations, country-based movements like Hamas and Hezbollah, transnational movements like the Muslim Brotherhood, and local community groups that operate at neighborhood level; and, (d) the reasons why a few Islamist movements adopt political violence and military resistance, while the vast majority of such movements that speak in a religious vocabulary are non-violent.

Politics and nationalism, rather than religion and spirituality per se, are the major drivers of Islamist movements. Journalists in the Western world should embrace their compelling legacies of political independence, ideological honesty, and technical professionalism to cover the big story that they largely have missed to date: the intersection between religion, politics, and nationalism, and these forces' occasional encounter with terrorism and violence.

A good entry point to this story in Arab-Islamic lands would be to recall how political violence and terror intersected with national and political issues in Northern Ireland and South Africa, for example, and how the violence ended when underlying political, national, and socio-economic grievances were addressed in a manner that both sides found to be fair and satisfactory. Closer to home in the United States is the legacy of politics and religion in the civil rights movement, where the Rev. Martin Luther King, Jr. and fellow clergy led the revolt against institutionalized racism. More recent examples of how ordinary men and women turn to their religion to fight political oppression were the demonstrating Buddhist monks in Myanmar, or the millions of young Iranians who shouted "Allahuakbar" (God is great) from their rooftops in the evenings during the revolt against the Iranian government in mid-2009.

The world urgently needs a more comprehensive, integrated, nuanced, and accurate analysis of the linkages among the important phenomena of nationalism, religion, identity, terrorism, politics, and resistance. The critical first step is disaggregating these different issues, and understanding when they converge and when they diverge. It is understandable to a large extent that Western media emphasize the association of Islam with violence, given the massive coverage of the terror that has become such a common and disfiguring part of some Muslim-majority societies. It would be the same if a discussion of modern anti-Semitism ended up talking mostly about Christian Europe and Russia, where this scourge was born and reached its peaks.

Some historical issues are associated indelibly with specific regions of the world, as terrorism and Islamic societies often are linked in the public eye in our times. In fact, it may be useful to start the quest for a more accurate understanding of Islam, nationalism, and violence by focusing on the many dimensions in which Islam the religion manifests itself in the lives of individuals and entire societies.

An overview of Islam and Islamist political trends should acknowledge six elements that sometimes converge, but often do not:

- Islam the religion, which has many varieties and dimensions around the world (Sunni, Shiite, Sufi, etc.);

- Muslims as individual men and women who seek the comfort of dignified citizenship within stable statehood, as citizens of countries in every part of the world;

- Islamism as a widespread phenomenon of political mobilization and expression anchored in explicit values, and that transcends countries and religious movements (similar to Christian fundamentalists in North America,

Europe, Asia, and Africa who are similarly motivated by a common religious zeal that often finds expression in organized politics at a national level);

- Nationalist Islamists who operate within their own country, with a view to liberating themselves from foreign occupation or changing state policies (Justice and Development Party in Turkey, Hamas in Palestine, Hezbollah in Lebanon, Taliban in Afghanistan, etc.);

- Social and community Islamism that sees individuals living their lives and organizing their local communities according to Islamic dictates of justice, modesty, compassion, and generosity; and

- Salafist[2] militants and terrorists like al-Qaeda and smaller groups that have sprung up around the world, that see themselves fighting a global defensive jihad to protect the Islamic Umma (community) from foreign domination or internal subversion and corruption.

There is no such thing as a single "Islam," or common attitudes among Muslims, that can be diagnosed, analyzed, or engaged as a monolithic whole. It is a sign of deep ignorance for headline writers or profound ideological rage for people to use phrases like, "What's wrong with Islam?"; "Why do they hate us?"; or "Islam and the West." For journalists, it is also a sign of laziness or amateurism.

The variety and dynamism of changes have been staggering in recent years, both in Islamic societies and in the hearts and minds of individual Muslims. This is understandable, given the intensity of the degradation that many Muslim-majority societies have suffered in the past half century of foreign manipulation, domestic mismanagement and abuse of political power, and local deterioration of social, environmental, and economic conditions. Religion in its many dimensions has been a common aspect of how ordinary citizens and organized movements respond to their predicaments of autocracy, poverty, occupation, or political stress.

The six different forms of Islamist identity and expression mentioned above evolve constantly, reflecting changing realities at the local level in most cases. Turkey has become the world's most impressive democratic, constitutional, and largely secular Muslim-majority society and one of the few where the military and security forces are largely under civilian oversight. Egypt, on the other hand, sees Islamism spread throughout society mostly in the form of the increasing piety of individuals and the activism of groups at the community level—while Islamist parties like the Muslim Brotherhood engage in formal politics, knowing very well that the military-dominated ruling elite will always control policy. Every country is different, and Islamist religious politics respond accordingly in different ways around the world.

The overwhelming majority of Muslims and Islamist groups have rejected the violent strategy of the small Salafist militants such as al-Qaeda. Yet it is also troubling that the core grievances of both the militants and the non-violent majority are virtu-ally identical. Good journalists and political analysts would acknowledge and act on that distinction, while merchants of hate, ignorance, and revenge ignore the distinc-tions and lump Islam and violence into a single phenomenon. Salafist militants decide to bomb foreigners and Muslims alike, but the majority of disgruntled Muslims deal with their predicament of imprecise citizenship rights in often unstable and corrupt societies by trying to lead more pious lives, while challenging the status quo and the power elite as they can.

Individual Muslims express or practice their faith in a wide variety of ways, from introspective personal spiritualism, through public social or political action, to the small extreme of violent militants. The overwhelming majority of Muslims and Is-lamist groups have responded to their individual and national predicaments with pa-tience, rationality, and non-violence. Most — individuals and movements alike — seek to advance the core values they cherish, including justice, equality, accountability, rule of law, compassion, and mercy. The handfuls of criminals and anarchists in the Is-lamic world should not detract from the reasonable aims of the majority any more than anti-Semites should be allowed to define the entirety of Christian Europeans.

Islamist political, nationalist, social, and religious movements have operated in the Arab-Asian region since the birth of Islam over 14 centuries ago. Islamist politi-cal movements tend to reassert themselves in different forms every several centuries, as societies constantly strive to find the balance between their religious values and their nationalist or political configurations. The most recent wave of Islamist politics in the Middle East started in the 1970s, driven by reactions to the excesses of the oil boom of that decade and by the Islamic revolution that overthrew the Shah of Iran in 1979. Developments around the Middle East and the wider Islamic realm in the past three decades now indicate that the broad movement of "political Islam" has settled down into three general trends. Al-Qaeda-style terror-warriors are the smallest but most dangerous group, provoking strong American-led military responses around the world. The middle group in terms of size and impact comprises Iran and allied, predominantly Shiite, Arab movements in Iraq, Lebanon, and other lands. They focus on self-empowerment and resisting what they see as the hegemonic aims of the United States and Israel. The third and largest group is made up of predominantly Sunni mainstream Islamists: Hamas, Muslim Brotherhood, the Turkish, Justice and Development Party — who increasingly engage in electoral democratic politics, at local and national governance levels.

The wide variety of Islamists includes movements with very different goals and tactics, but almost everywhere they are spurred initially by local conditions, stresses, and grievances. These are evolving rather than static movements, constantly re-sponding to domestic and external stimuli, but always accountable to their home con-stituencies if they plan to survive and prevail. In a few crucial areas their motivations overlap, though their operational and strategic goals usually differ. They are likely to reconfigure their relationships and alliances in the future, especially in response to external meddling.

The range of issues and responses that define the varied world of Islamist politics can be seen in the news during a typical week in 2008: Osama bin Laden released another threatening audio message. The next day, three bombs exploded in an Egyptian tourist resort. Turkey's mild Islamist government confronted complex challenges of Kurdish militancy and separatism, growing Turkish nationalism, and a democratic transformation required to meet the terms of joining the European Union. Palestine's elected government headed by Hamas was threatened at home by its rival Fateh, and by siege and strangulated from abroad by the United States, Europe, and Israel. The Iranian government built on its announcement of mastering small-scale uranium enrichment by defying and provoking the West and Israel, who are trying to prevent its development of a full nuclear fuel cycle. Hezbollah in Lebanon continued to flex its muscles as the largest and best organized Lebanese political group that is also close to Iran and Syria, but faces increasingly vocal calls for its disarmament or incorporation into the national armed forces. Mainstream Muslim Brotherhood-style movements in Egypt, Jordan, Morocco, and most other Arab countries continued to explore how they can engage in democratic elections in order to share or control power, without being outlawed or emasculated.

Shared Grievances

The common denominator among all the Islamist trends is their shared sense of grievances against three primary targets, in their eyes: autocratic Arab regimes that run security states usually dominated by a handful of members of a single family; Israel and its negative impact on Arab societies, through direct occupations or indirect political influence on U.S. policy in the region; and, the United States and other Western powers whose military and political interference in the Middle East is widely seen as a threat to the majority of people in the region.

The three most prominent strands of Islamist activism are represented broadly by non-violent mass organizations or groups like the Muslim Brotherhood of Egypt, national resistance and empowerment movements like Hezbollah, and a handful of terrorist groups like al-Qaeda. They have responded variously to these grievances by fostering a combination of ideological defiance of the West, armed resistance against Israeli and American occupation forces, and political challenges to Arab regimes. They part ways, however, when it comes to tactics and methods: Al-Qaeda blows up targets around the world; the Iranian-Arab-Shiite groups focus on empowered political resistance and defiance often wrapped in revolutionary rhetoric; and, Sunni mainstreamers resist militarily when appropriate (Hamas in Palestine) but more often concentrate on playing and winning the political game on the strength of their numbers and organization, Turkey being their most impressive performance to date.

Throughout the Middle East and other Islamic lands, citizens who seek to become politically involved to change their world have these three options of Islamist assertion and activism before them. Two of them—bin Ladenist terror and Iranian-led defiance—are being fought fiercely by the West, and also by some people in the region. The third option of democratic electoral politics is at a major crossroads, following the Hamas victory in Palestine, Hezbollah's strong governance role in Lebanon, and the prominence of the Muslim Brotherhood in Egypt.

Should mainstream peaceful political Islamism be killed and buried, the subsequent landscape very well could see a coming together of five powerful forces that overwhelmingly dominate the political cultures of the Middle East, and that until now generally had been kept separate: Sunni Islamic religious militancy, Arab national sentiment, anti-occupation military resistance, Iranian-Persian nationalism, and regional Shiite empowerment among Arabs and Iranians. These forces have tended to operate separately, but form temporary or long-term alliances when it is mutually advantageous to do so. They are also all primarily political, communal, or nationalist movements, but they find their most potent expression within a religious organizational context and vocabulary.

In the realm of transnational movements that have attracted a very small number of followers but carry out spectacular terror attacks that generate the most attention and media coverage, the best known is al-Qaeda. Just over two decades ago it was born in Afghanistan, as a movement of zealous holy warriors that was prepared to fight and die to protect the Islamic umma, or community, from foreign assault. The Russian occupation of Afghanistan was the immediate catalyst that sparked its creation, though the formative motivations sending thousands of young men from Arab and Asian lands to join the jihad were usually anchored in local events and personal experiences.

The several phenomena that al-Qaeda represents—defensive jihad, militant self-assertion, a puritanical interpretation of religious doctrine, cosmic theological battle, and political struggle to purify tainted Islamic societies—appeal to a variety of individuals who gravitate to its call in the same manner that zealots join any other such cult-like movement of true believers, zealots, and fanatics. Coming to grips with the phenomena it represents—especially the continuing threat of terrorism—requires looking beyond al-Qaeda's surface expression of militant self-defense of threatened or occupied Islamic lands; it requires grasping the combination of social, economic, and political conditions in local societies from which al-Qaeda recruits emanate. These come mainly from Arab societies, but also from South Asia and immigrant quarters of urban Europe.

Al-Qaeda's entry into its third decade of life is an appropriate moment to do this. A longer, 20-plus-years analytical time frame is far more useful than the shorter period commemorating the September 11 attack against the United States that was al-Qaeda's signature event. Since 1989, al-Qaeda has evolved in line with trends impacting the wider world of Islamist movements, including local crackdowns in many countries, and the American-led "global war on terror" that has been defined heavily, but not exclusively, by the wars in Afghanistan and Iraq. These pressures to disrupt al-Qaeda have been offset by a continuation of the stressful conditions at local and national levels in many Arab-Asian societies that nourish these Salafist jihadi movements in the first place.

It is important always to ask about al-Qaeda's condition today; it is far more important to understand the wider trends in Arab-Asian societies that bolster Islamist radicalism, because of five related conditions that drive disaffected young men into the arms of militant groups:

1. The slow political fragmentation and fraying at the edges of once-centralized nation-states like Pakistan, Iraq, Somalia, Lebanon, Palestine, Sudan, Yemen, Afghanistan, and Algeria, creating vacuums of authority that Islamists and others quickly fill.
2. The continued sharp disparities in local delivery of basic social services, job opportunities, and security throughout much of the Arab-Asian region, creating urgent needs that Islamists are very good at meeting.
3. The impact of major nationalist issues such as the Arab-Israeli conflict or the Anglo-American-led war on Iraq.
4. Police brutality and political oppression at the local level in many Arab-Asian countries (the birthplace of al-Qaeda was both Afghanistan and the prisons of Egypt).
5. Occasional external, and mostly Western, stimuli to those who see themselves fighting a defensive jihad to protect both the honor and the physical existence of the threatened Islamic umma. Examples of such external "threats" include the Danish cartoons, Pope Benedict's speech in August 2006, virulently anti-Islamic movies and books, and a tendency by leading politicians (including American presidential candidates and leading television personalities) to repeatedly speak of an undefined "Islamic radicalism" as a great threat to Western civilization that must be fought for decades, if not lifetimes.

The combination of these factors slowly but persistently has fomented two generations of Islamist activists who have mostly joined peaceful movements like the Muslim Brotherhood. Small numbers have split off and embraced fringe militant and terrorist groups. Much debate swirls around the condition and status of al-Qaeda, which has clearly suffered operational setbacks with the loss of its Afghan bases, but seems to have regrouped in the northwestern frontier areas of Pakistan where it has widespread support among Taliban-friendly communities. While al-Qaeda has been disrupted, other similar, smaller Salafist militant groups have sprung to life in Iraq, Somalia, Lebanon, Yemen, Algeria, and elsewhere.

Any militant movement that endures for more than 20 years and spurs dozens of smaller clones is not only a consequence of its own organizational prowess. It reflects the persistence of enabling conditions that breed militants and militancy. Reducing the threat of terrorism from groups such as al-Qaeda requires that we understand and work to ameliorate the wider degrading conditions that feed recruits into terror movements—including, most notably, packed jails, socio-economic disparity, and abuse of power in the Arab world; long-term Israeli occupations and colonization of Arab lands; Anglo-American wars; and, Western Islamophobia.

Understanding Hamas

Unlike al-Qaeda which is the exception to the rule, the vast majority of Islamist movements are born, and grow in strength, within a distinctly nationalist context in a single country. They have strategic and tactical links with others beyond their frontiers, but at their core they are state-centered and local movements that know and respond to their constituents and their needs. Hezbollah in Lebanon and Hamas in Palestine are two of the best examples of movements that were born in the 1980s and have since grown to the point where they share in national governance and in some aspects (military resistance to Israeli occupation), they are more powerful than the government and the national armed forces.

Israel, the United States, and some other countries reject dealing with Hamas because they see it purely as a terrorist organization dedicated to the "destruction of Israel." The reality is more complex. Hamas certainly has committed acts of terror against Israeli civilians, and it must be held accountable for such deeds. This ideally should be in a context in which all who commit murder and terror in the Middle East are similarly held accountable, including Israelis, Arabs, Iranians, Americans, and British. Hamas argues that its actions are legitimate resistance in the context of a much more brutal Israeli war against Palestinians—one that it says includes Israeli state terror, assassination, kidnapping, starvation, imprisonment, colonization, siege, collective punishment, apartheid-like segregation, and other nasty policies. The nature of Hamas's political and military confrontation with Israel will be debated for many years. More useful would be to explore the underlying reasons for Hamas's strength and credibility in its own society, with a view to understanding if Hamas can be a legitimate political partner in a negotiation to achieve a permanent resolution of the Arab-Israeli conflict.

This important issue may hold the key to progress toward true peace. It would also help generate a more accurate, comprehensive understanding of how these Islamist movements combine religion, nationalism, politics, and identity into a single movement that generates millions of followers. This requires assessing and engaging

Hamas and other Islamists on the same basis that was used in the case of other militant or terrorist groups around the world, including the IRA in Northern Ireland, the Viet Cong in Vietnam, SWAPO in Namibia, the ANC in South Africa, and, more recently, the "insurgents" in Iraq, and the Taliban in Afghanistan and Pakistan. All eventually became political interlocutors and negotiating partners in processes that brought an end to long-running conflicts.

Such an approach typically comprises four critical components: Talk to the groups in question rather than boycott them; make clear their objectionable and unacceptable actions that must stop; identify their legitimate nationalistic or political demands that can be met; and, negotiate in a context of equality to achieve a win-win situation that stops the political violence and terror, removes the underlying reasons for it, satisfies all sides' minimum demands and rights, and achieves peace and security. If one were to seek a peaceful win-win situation with Hamas, for example, one would have to engage it within the total context of all its principles, motivations, and actions, and not only through the narrow lens of violent or terror acts.

Hamas's worldview and political program together explain why it has grown in popularity by responding to the needs of its fellow Palestinians living under Israeli occupation. These can be summarized as fighting to resist occupation and liberate occupied land; resolve the core refugee problem of the Palestinians; create an orderly, secure, and non-corrupt society; deliver efficient government services; be treated internationally with respect; and not be subjected to double standards by foes or great powers. These are overwhelmingly political and nationalist issues, not primarily religious ones. Hamas's religious values and sentiments reflect commitment to a life and society defined by the values common to the Abrahamic faiths, including justice, peace, generosity, mercy, compassion, and tolerance. Hamas's operative strength and credibility in society emanate partly from this adherence to religious values, but far more importantly to its commitment to work and, if need be, fight, for the basic rights that Palestinians demand.

Hezbollah's Many Roles

Hezbollah in Lebanon mirrors most of these same forces that define Hamas' success in Palestine, but it also allows us to understand how local or national Islamists enhance their positions through regional alliances. This transforms them from purely local actors to players on a wider stage, in this case the new Cold War in the Middle East between forces loosely allied either to the United States or to the Iran-Syria axis. Many people in Lebanon and abroad see Hezbollah mainly as a political or even military extension of Iranian and Syrian interests, and they now challenge it openly.

The Hezbollah situation is intriguing, and reflective of realities throughout this region, because it is so much more complex and multi-faceted. It is too simplistic to accuse Hezbollah of being a terrorist movement, an arm of Iran, an agent that Syria can manipulate, or any of the other attributes that it has been given. Hezbollah in fact has played a dozen important roles in its history, and these roles keep evolving, while some disappear to be replaced by others. Like Hamas and other Islamist political groups throughout the Middle East that have played a significant role in resisting foreign occupation or domestic autocrats, Hezbollah also recognizes that its future is likely to see it deeply engaged in domestic politics, mainly representing national constituencies in governance systems based on democratic elections.

Throughout its short life of a quarter of a century, Hezbollah's credibility and power have rested on five broad pillars: (1) delivering basic social welfare needs mainly to Shiite communities in different parts of Lebanon; (2) resisting and ending the Israeli occupation of southern Lebanon; (3) being part of the Iranian-inspired pan-Islamic movement that also challenges American "hegemonic" aims; (4) providing efficient, non-corrupt good governance at the local level; and, (5) more recently, emerging as the main representative and protector of Shiite communal interests within Lebanon's explicitly sectarian and confessional political system. In the turbulent years since 2005, however, the five legs on which Hezbollah stood for decades have been changing, or disappearing in some cases. The Syrian withdrawal from Lebanon, Iran's increasing diplomatic angst vis-à-vis the West, the Israeli departure from South Lebanon in 2000, and recent international pressures via U.N. Security Council resolutions have forced Hezbollah to review and redefine its national role in Lebanon.

Hezbollah seems to recognize that it must continue the transition it has been making in recent years—from primarily an armed resistance to Israeli occupation and a service delivery body operating in the south, to a national political organization, sitting in parliament and the cabinet and operating on a national political stage. It is unrealistic to deal with Hezbollah as a one-dimensional group that is only an armed resistance force, a political adjunct of Iran, a friend of Syria, the main interlocutor for Shiites in Lebanese politics and power-sharing, a growing force in parliament, or an Islamist voice of global, anti-imperialist resistance. It is all these things, and always has been. It is also an important supporter of Palestinians in their struggle for liberation and statehood, a leading proponent of the blend between Islamism and Arabism, a rare case of Arabs liberating their lands from Israeli occupation and driving away foreign forces, and an example of efficient, methodical strategic planning and careful implementation in both local and regional policies. Local or global parties, who want to nudge it toward more involvement in national democratic politics, and away from political and armed militancy, should resist the simplistic tendency to paint it—or any other group—in one-dimensional terms that are politically convenient, but factually and historically incomplete or just plain wrong.

The nuances and complexities of Hezbollah's status are important for Lebanon, but they also mirror a range of related issues throughout the Middle East: What are the Islamist movements' ultimate domestic aims? What is the real balance among their religiosity, nationalism, resistance, communal empowerment, and politics? How do ties with Iran play in Arab circles? Is the Syrian-Iranian-led "resistance front" against the U.S.-Israel-Arab conservatives the way of the future, or a cruel deception from the past? How far can armed struggle go in the battle against Israel, before the U.S.-Israel combine uses devastating force to turn threatening neighbors into wastelands of total destruction—and would such destruction have any long-term impact?

The mainstream Western media and political elites—especially in the United States—continue to ignore the considerable nuances and ever-changing realities of Islamist-nationalist groups like Hezbollah. The tendency in much of the Arab-Islamic world is to go to the other extreme, of seeing Hezbollah as a valiant, inerrant force for righteousness, self-respect, and powerful Arab and Islamic self-assertion. The truth, as always, is at neither extreme.

Provenance tells us much about the core aims and values of movements like Hamas and Hezbollah, both of which did not exist before the early 1980s. Their birth and strength must be understood largely as a response to Israel's occupation and colonization policies in Palestine and Lebanon, alongside their other roles mentioned above. Another common trait to both groups is about the convergence among religion, nationalism, governance, and politics. In both Palestine and Lebanon, the prevailing secular political systems proved dysfunctional, corrupt, and unable to protect the society against Israeli aggression or domestic strife and criminality. Movements like Hamas and Hezbollah developed in large part to fill the vacuum in efficient governance, security against Israeli attacks, and domestic order. They have achieved mixed results, with success in some areas but also an intensification of warfare and destruction in others.

Trying to discredit these movements by accusing them of transgression—for example, they use terrorism, attack civilians, carry arms, cozy up to Syria and Iran, espouse an Islamist agenda—is unlikely to discredit or destroy them, as Israel and some Arab parties that oppose them have learned in recent decades. This is because of the structural manner in which they fulfill multiple roles that respond to the needs of their citizens and constituents in the realms of governance, local security, national defense, and basic service delivery—responsibilities that their secular national governments often failed to fulfill. Hezbollah and Hamas in their current configuration are Islamist-nationalist movements that act on a long list of grievances that must be addressed if peace and security are ever to reign in the Middle East. A good starting point for journalists would be to recognize the multiple dimensions of Islamist movements in the Middle East, where nationalism, religion, politics, identity, and military resistance blend together so seamlessly that foreign observers tend to miss the seams that connect the many other dimensions beyond religion and militancy.

These complex conditions have challenged journalists in the past, and will do so in the future. In the realm of press, religion, and politics, worthy goals are to have better informed world citizens, and to have accurate information for policymakers appear in news reports.

SUGGESTED DISCUSSION QUESTIONS

1. What does the author perceive to be the biggest challenge facing Western journalists in understanding Islamist movements? How does the author suggest using history as a way of developing more understanding?

2. Discuss the three strands of Islamist activism and how they differ.

3. What specifically are the stakes for any failure of peaceful political Islamism in the Mideast? The author identifies some forces that could come into play. What are they?

4. What are the characteristics of al-Qaeda as discussed by the author and what deeper realities need to be understood by journalists? What forces does he say draw people to militant groups?

5. In what key respect are most Islamist movements different from al-Qaeda?

6. What suggestion does the author have for understanding Hamas and for constructive engagement with it?

7. Discuss the complexity the author sees in Hezbollah's alliances, its regional view, and domestic aims.

ENDNOTES

1. See the website of the Chicago Project on Security and Terrorism, http://cpost.uchicago.edu/, in particular Pape's testimony to a Congressional hearing on Afghanistan policy on October 22, 2009, (http://armedservices.house.gov/pdfs/TUTC102209/Pape_TestimonyF102209.pdf).

2. Salafist (or Salafi) refers to the strict and narrow interpretation of Islamic principles and practices that purport to emulate the earliest generation of Muslims at the time of the Prophet Mohammad and shortly thereafter. This is something akin to militant fundamentalists among Christians, including those Christians who use violence against practices such as abortion.

CHAPTER 3

Lessons from Iraq: Religion and the Journalism of International Relations

Jack Miles

The author is distinguished professor of English and Religious Studies at UC-Irvine, and Senior Fellow for Religious Affairs with the Pacific Council on International Policy. His writing has appeared in The Atlantic, the New York Times, the Washington Post, the Los Angeles Times, the Boston Globe, *and many other publications. His book* God: A Biography *won a Pulitzer Prize in 1996. His book,* Christ: A Crisis in the Life of God, *led to his being named a MacArthur Fellow for the years 2003–2007. He currently is at work as general editor of the forthcoming Norton Anthology of World Religions.*

In covering international news, just as in domestic news, every reporter, editor, and commentator begins with what in philosophy would be called a heuristic, from the Greek verb *heurein,* "to discover." The classic "who, what, when, where, and sometimes why" is a heuristic, with the "sometimes" bespeaking the once-revolutionary determination of editorial leadership to segregate news from opinion, reportage from commentary. In print media, now that who, what, when, and where are more rapidly delivered by other media, classic editorial opinion has been joined by "analysis," the fifth W now migrated to the front page in a modified form. Unfortunately for the American republic, the other media have radically reduced their commitment to the first four Ws; talk radio has been joined by talk television in a kind of triumph of commentary over reporting.

Whatever the future health or configuration of news media, the reporting and interpretation of international news will remain difficult for the same reason that international relations themselves are difficult—namely, that each culture specifies the five Ws in its own way. Working in a foreign country, whether in the Marine Corps, the Peace Corps, or the diplomatic corps, you think you know, at least, *what* you are doing. Sometimes, though, you discover (*heurein*) that your hosts understand you to be doing something else. You think you are rescuing orphans, for example; they think you are buying and selling children.

The point is a simple one and an old one, alive in a thousand proverbs and in every language: *Autres pays, autres moeurs;* one man's meat is another man's poison, and so forth. And yet a point so easily grasped in theory is just as easy to forget in practice. How does one realistically approximate accurate perception and avoid culturally induced misperception? One does so, I submit, by appending to the classic five questions as informed and extensive a check-list of sub-questions as one can develop.

A few entries are obvious: sex, money, knowledge. In a tale from Greek mythology,[1] Paris, a mortal, is required to judge which of three goddesses is the fairest. Hera promises to make him the most powerful man in the world if he awards her the golden apple. Athena promises to make him the smartest. Aphrodite promises him the love of the most beautiful woman in the world. Aphrodite wins, the woman is Helen of Troy, and the rest is Homeric history.

Can a nation go to war because of a woman? In Christopher Marlowe's immortal words, "Was this the face that launched a thousand ships / And burnt the topless towers of Ilium?"[2] A skeptic would say no. It wasn't really sex. It was really something else. Some love-affairs are about money. Some are about social climbing. Some are about trophy-wife or trophy-escort ambition. But some are about love, or even simply lust. Sexual hunger is an independent variable in the affairs of the smart and powerful. Again and again, we see them make the choice that Paris made—and pay the price. Careers collapse, empires disintegrate, and the skeptical media are taken by surprise. It shouldn't have happened. It did. They should have been ready for it. They weren't.

The remarks that follow amount to a plea that news reporters and commentators, especially when considering societies other than our own, be ready to see religion as no less independent a variable than sex. Journalists should be as ready to see rational calculations of self-interest overridden by religion as by sex. They should be watching. They should be ready. With the necessary discretion, they should be asking, and they should not *always* disbelieve what they hear.

Fortune favors the prepared mind. Astute asking makes all the difference, and one must formulate a question for oneself before posing it to a potential news source or about a potential news subject. Because in our culture religion is for many as private a matter as sex, because the scope of its role in public life is sharply limited, we tend to expect privacy and a similarly limited public scope to be its place of religion in other cultures as well. The result for journalism is both that we too discreetly (one might almost say religiously) refrain from asking intrusive questions about religion—

questions, that is, which we would find intrusive—and that we too readily assume that in so doing we neglect nothing of public importance.

I do not mean to exaggerate the importance of religion. In no society that I know of are religious motives the only effective motives. Yet the cross-cultural mistake most easily made by diplomats or journalists from a secular culture attempting to relate to or report on a religious culture (and most of the cultures of the world *are* religious) is to read allegedly religious motivation as disguised motivation of some other sort. Greed, lust, ambition, and religious devotion are not mutually exclusive passions. But we must not assume that any one of them is reducible to the others. Just as sometimes it really is lust, or love, sometimes it really is fervor, or faith.

Coverage of the second Gulf War, now usually just called the War in Iraq, presents an instructive example. Following the classic five-W heuristic, a foreign correspondent could and properly should ask before landing in Baghdad: Who are the Iraqis? If we assume that Iraqi identity, like most national identity, has several component parts, which part is most important? If Iraqi identity were a card game, which card would be trump? Former President George W. Bush and his Democratic opponents alike seemed to believe at the outset of the war that nationality was the trump card. To admit as a real possibility that religion might be trump—that is, that being Muslim or, more to the point, being Sunni or Shiite was trump—would be to admit the possibility that the war could not be won on the terms the president had set, no matter how long it lasted and how bravely American soldiers fought. If the Americans were fighting neither for the Sunni nor for the Shiites but for both as equally Iraqi by birth, while on religious grounds neither of these equally Iraqi populations was prepared to make peace with the other, then the American forces would necessarily be fighting on both sides of a religious civil war. They would be fighting themselves, with no prospect of victory.

In the months and years since the end of the Bush administration, a chastened awareness of the power of the religious component in all Middle Eastern identities—a matter all but unmentioned in the debate that preceded the war—may at least mitigate the grave consequences of the American withdrawal now somewhat haltingly under way. For American journalism to foster this awareness, what is called for, fortunately, is not some preternatural cultural sensitivity that will enable a reporter to divine what all others, including his country's diplomatic corps and executive leadership, have missed. Moments of prescience and brilliance do come, but they are not the norm.

The norm for attainable excellence should be a reporter or commentator's valorization of information that is available with only a little searching but has been undervalued or muted for extrinsic, often political reasons. In explaining why the elder Bush administration had not carried the fighting to Baghdad and overthrown Saddam Hussein in the first Gulf War, Richard Cheney, secretary of defense in that administration, showed a clear awareness of the fault lines in Iraqi society that made the larger war unwinnable.[3]

One may fault the Democratic opposition to the second Gulf War, but one may more sharply fault the media. Had they more accurately reported the virulence and ominous recentness of the Kurd/Arab and Sunni/Shiite hostility, the congressional debate scarcely could have avoided these highly relevant topics. It was not Saddam Hussein personally who had brutally suppressed the Shiites before the first Gulf War and even more brutally suppressed them after it when—deceived by American encouragement—they rose in rebellion against him. It was not Hussein alone who had attempted genocide against the Kurds. These actions were undertaken, in the first case, by one ethnic minority against another and, in the second, by one Muslim sect against another. All this was a matter of vividly living Iraqi memory in Iraq at the time when the United States launched the second Gulf War. Was it not predictable, then, that the overthrow of the dictator would unleash an orgy of revenge that a foreign power like the United States, whose troops do not speak the local languages, could not easily control?

Unfortunately, instead of foregrounding this question in all coverage of the impending war or the first months of the occupation, the media generally acquiesced in the official U.S. view that, if and when Saddam Hussein could be overthrown, the liberated Iraqis would let bygones by bygones and would work peacefully together *as* Iraqis to build their "young democracy" and improve its standard of living. Why would they ever surrender life and fortune to religious or ethnic vendetta? That shouldn't have happened. It did happen. The media should have been ready. They weren't.

The utterly unintended but fatefully consequential effect of the war has been the transformation of Iraq into the first Shiite-ruled Arab state to have come into existence in centuries. This new state is on religious grounds as well as many practical grounds a natural ally of Iran, a sworn enemy of the United States in fighting whom the United States had once been willing to assist even the reviled Saddam Hussein.

This is the Iraq that the Obama administration hopes to stabilize by encouraging the Shiite Arab majority to make due accommodation of Iraq's Sunni Arab and Sunni Kurd minorities. Whether or not this interfaith, interethnic hope can be realized, one can only note that, even now, American journalism engages the subject of the real ethnic or religious differences involved. Instead of these terms, the terms invoked by the Obama administration are still the resolutely secular, political terms favored by the second Bush administration, with only intermittent challenge by the media.

The Iraq war was not sold to the American people as a war against the Sunni on behalf of the Shiites, or against the Arabs on behalf of the Kurds. It was sold as a war of American self-defense, first, and, second, as the liberation of all Iraqis from the tyrannical Saddam Hussein. Americans were encouraged to believe that, without any real examination of evidence, Iraqis thought of themselves as Iraqi first and only then as Kurd, Sunni Arab, or Shiite Arab. Meanwhile, in much the same vein, Hussein was never engaged as the commander of a large and powerful faction within Iraq. Instead, he was seen in isolation and always spoken of in the demonic singular: "He" refused to surrender "his" weapons of mass destruction, though we had given "him" every chance to do so. The ruling Baath Party, Hussein's party, nominally secular but in fact overwhelmingly Sunni, was never spoken of as a significant part of the population which had to be stripped of its ascendency over the remainder of the population. Among the Sunni Arabs of Iraq, the dominance of the Tikriti clan, Hussein's clan, lavishly favored within his regime, was never mentioned either.

A Marine colonel once shared with me the brilliantly concise justification for the war that he gave his men as they faced first combat: "We are here to give Iraq back to the Iraqis." I call his formulation brilliant because it put in a single sentence the rationale for the war offered by America's political leadership. Unstated but assumed, just as the Bush administration had done, whatever Vice President Cheney knew to the contrary, was that the Iraqis were as united as the Americans or the Mexicans or the Canadians, that they were not engaged in anything like an interrupted religious war, and that their oppression was by one man of the entire population rather than by one large, religiously defined minority of the majority.

That vision of what the war was and is "all about" has generally lived on in the press no less than in Congress whenever talk has been heard of putting pressure on "the Iraqis." The possibility of such pressure—to pass oil legislation, for example, or to schedule a postponed referendum or to introduce nonsectarian recruitment to the army—rests on the assumption that there exists now and has always existed a silent majority of "plain" Iraqis for whom, in the American way, racial, ethnic, and, above all, religious differences are effectively subordinated to patriotic allegiance. These were the Iraqis to whom former President Bush referred when he said, as he repeatedly did: "When they stand up, we will stand down." But when they stood up, they were found to be shooting at each other with American-supplied guns, firing weapons that they had been taught to fire by American-supplied advisors. How then could the United States emerge with a victory?

What the United States imagines itself to be doing even now for "the Iraqis" and against "the terrorists" is read differently, each time out, by the Shiites or Sunni whose interests happen to be served or not. Sunni read actions that benefit Shiites as anti-Sunni or, more likely, simply anti-Islam. Shiites read actions that benefit Sunni in the same way. The elections that so cheered the former president brought a Shiite majority into the legislature, and that majority proceeded to serve Shiite interests to the point that the Sunni bloc repeatedly boycotted the legislature. Shiites, who outnumber Sunni in the military as they do in the population at large, have created an army that may sometimes protect Shiite civilians against Sunni terrorism but rarely punishes Shiite terrorists who attack Sunni civilians.

The result? Much of the Sunni populace, to this day, regards the "Iraqi" army as an enemy army, a point essentially conceded in a White House progress report released on July 12, 2007. Prime Minister Maliki never overcame his fear that the Bush administration "surge" was creating Sunni militias that, like the Taliban in Afghanistan after the Soviet withdrawal, would turn against his government after the American withdrawal. Spectacular terror-bombings in mid-2009 Iraq suggest that his fears were not groundless. Depending on where they are and on whom among the contending Iraqi groups they are found supporting, U.S. forces may come under attack even by Iraqis whom they have personally trained, a development that would be ludicrous if it were not so utterly demoralizing.

My point is not to choose sides in a religious dispute, only to note the relevance of the dispute itself to the understanding of Iraq and the prospects of success for any intervening foreign power. Knowing the bitter and recent history of interreligious and interethnic conflict in Iraq, the Coalition Provisional Authority was naïve to permit elections in which parties were allowed to compete *as* Shiites or Sunni for offices that ignored the tribal structure that had complicated, blurred, and thus moderated the polarizing power of religious difference. Effective resistance to al-Qaeda in Iraq arose in Falluja via a rehabilitation of the tribal structure in new kinds of cooperation with the American military that tacitly ignored the Iraqi constitution.

Tribalism, clearly, can be a source of fanatic violence, and so can sectarianism. But substitute nationalism for tribalism, and religious devotion for sectarianism, and these terms subside into something that, after all, we need not regard as utterly alien. The responsible journalist must begin from the premise that the relationship of civil and religious elements differs from any one society to the next, that most complex social arrangements have latent functions that an outsider is particularly likely to miss, and that for this reason large disruptions of a social order—as must always be the case with a military invasion—are inherently error-prone and risky.

Iraq's tribes, especially in the not infrequent case when interreligious marriage had created substantially bi-sectarian, Sunni-Shiite tribes, was a factor that employed family loyalty to mitigate the excesses of religious loyalty and began to bring down the levels of Iraqi sectarian violence. The United States, by creating a secular government whose divisions overrode tribal borders and tribal authorities, and by then licensing religiously defined parties to compete for the newly created offices, supercharged the power of religion to undermine civilian order as a whole.

Greater attention to religion as a major factor determining the character of Iraqi political life necessarily would have involved greater attention to factors that, from within Iraq itself, mitigated the power of religion. Greater attention by the press to this interaction could have helped the often-scorned diplomatic corps "sell" the relevance of this interaction to the American public.

Tribalism, to repeat, can create conflict as easily as religion can. From the outset, Iraq's religious civil war has been twinned by an ethnic conflict between Sunni Arabs and Sunni Kurds over oil-rich northern Iraqi territories. Nationality trumps religion in that conflict inasmuch as both local parties to it are Sunni. Unfortunately, there are two nationalities in play. The Kurds regard Iraqi nationality not as ethnically neutral but as a species of Arab nationality, the nationality of those who attempted genocide against the Kurds in the 1980s. This, too, was common knowledge before the American invasion and portended the greatest of difficulty in putting together an all-for-one-and-one-for-all Iraq, a multi-ethnic, religiously pluralist nation that would not need to be held together, as Saddam Hussein's Iraq was, only by main force.

In effect, the main force of the deposed dictator has been replaced by the main force of the American military. But whether or not Americans wish to play this role in perpetuity, few Iraqis wish them to play it. In Iraq's unfinished ethnic conflict as in its religious conflict, the United States cannot win by backing one side against the other. It cannot easily bring the Iraqis to make peace with each other by mere persuasion. But its worst of all possible options was to back — and arm — all sides at once. That policy can only make a bloody stalemate even bloodier. Awareness of this may explain why so many Iraqis, in repeated polls, say they want the Americans out.

It is not that there are no secular Iraqi nationalists willing to subordinate religious and ethnic differences in the formation of a common political identity and the pursuit of such common interests as the equitable development of Iraq's crucial oil resources. But their number is small, and their weak influence was further weakened by the failure of the occupying forces quickly to establish basic security and reliable working condition. During the New York City blackout of July 13, 1977, I was living in New York, and I vividly recall that the sound of breaking glass — the sound of a social order breaking down — began perhaps five minutes after the lights went out. The police sirens began to wail perhaps a minute after that and did not stop for many hours. When the lights came back on, order was restored and the looting stopped. But if the lights had kept going out? If they were out for hours every day? If, as happened under the Coalition Provisional Authority in Iraq, the police force had been disbanded while plans were made to hire a new one, less tainted by complicity with the abuses of an overthrown government? Then, I can easily believe, differences of race and class and even of religion that are now contained within the social order of New York might have become more lastingly virulent, and outsiders might have concluded that there was no hope in that city for a multiracial, multiethnic, religiously pluralist way of life. Unfortunately, though this observation may seem to place blame for the chaos in Iraq where it really belongs, it does not gainsay the fact that ongoing internecine religious and ethnic conflict in Iraq is now beyond reversal by any American success in providing essential services and basic security. The damage is incalculable, but the damage has been done.

At this juncture, the most the United States can hope to accomplish militarily in Iraq is to prevent the losing side in any conflict from losing too badly. American might is still sufficient to prevent civil war from escalating into genocide, even if it is not sufficient to impose peace. With that as a residual goal for Iraq and with the preservation of stability in the region and some continuation of American influence as residual goals for the United States itself, Congress now needs to look urgently *around* rather than just *at* Iraq and its region.

As a factor in Middle East politics, religion does not function in isolation, any more than it does so anywhere else in the world. Yet, however unreliable our instincts, American policymakers must learn to reckon at every point with the potential importance of religion as they attempt to stabilize the region, preserve American influence, and reduce Iraqi casualties during the American withdrawal.

In the interest of Kurdistan itself, as the one Iraqi region still in a position to snatch success from the jaws of the American failure, the United States must cooperate in the creation and funding of a robust Turkish-Kurdish border patrol aimed at keeping Kurdish revolutionaries out of Turkey and obviating the need for any Turkish incursion into Kurdistan. Turkish-American relations have been a major casualty of the Iraq war. Here may be an opportunity to repair them and, in the process, to maintain stability in an area crucial to the management of an orderly American withdrawal and to some continuation of American influence.

Moreover, it may well be in American interests to embrace the emerging moderately Islamic governing majority in Ankara, for its Sunni Islam, shared with the Kurds, seems to have moderated the conduct of Turkey's government toward the country's Kurdish minority, now represented for the first time in the Turkish parliament. For decades, nationality has aggressively trumped religion in Turkey, but it has done so at Kurdish expense. A benign acceptance of the coming change in Ankara may constitute a small step toward refuting the too common view in the Muslim world that the United States is conducting a war on Islam. Happily, by making Ankara the site of a promised first-hundred-days speech on relations between the United States and the Muslim world, President Obama dramatically raised the profile of religion as a legitimate topic within American diplomatic discourse and, accordingly, within American international journalism as well. The President's more far-reaching speech in Cairo did even more to make a legitimate subject of what had been for too long a non-subject.

East of Iraq, Shiite Iran has successfully withstood all international pressure to curtail its development of nuclear weapons and, despite the extraordinary turmoil that followed the 2009 Iranian presidential election, enjoys better relations with Iraqi Prime Minister Nuri al-Maliki than the Obama administration does. Should the tide turn against Iraq's Shiite-majority government in an escalating Sunni-Shiite Iraqi civil war, Iran would almost certainly follow Turkey's example and send its forces across the border. Before the war, it was assumed that age-old Persian/Arab enmity would trump Shiite solidarity between Iran and Iraq. By 2009, that assumption had been shaken if not thoroughly demolished. Congress must accept the bitter fact that the second Gulf War has massively strengthened Shiite Iran—already the third-strongest power in the region after Turkey and Israel—by turning a hostile Sunni neighbor, Iraq, into a friendly Shiite neighbor. Given this shift and despite the near civil war that erupted in Iran that after the rigged re-election of Mahmoud Ahmadinejad as president, peace with Iran even at the risk of offending Saudi Arabia and alarming Israel might well be a peace in the American interest. With the position in the Middle East now so badly weakened and the war in Afghanistan escalating steadily, this country cannot risk war with Iran.

South of Iraq, on the Persian Gulf island of Bahrain, where the U.S. Navy's Fifth Fleet is based, an oppressed Shiite majority threatens the ruling Sunni minority. The loss of Bahrain would cripple America's ability to wage any long-term war against Iran or even to service an "over the horizon" fallback force for Iraq. Looking ahead to withdrawal from Iraq and a fallback position in the region, Congress must take urgent thought for the future of Bahrain and for that of Qatar, another small Gulf state, which has hosted the headquarters of the U.S. Central Command. These taken-for-granted allies must be stabilized and protected if the United States is to retain any capacity to defend its interests.

South of Iraq but north of Qatar and Bahrain, Congress must face up to the unpleasant task of building a firewall around Kuwait, a Sunni-ruled principality surrounded, disliked, and threatened by nearby Shiites in its three larger neighbors (including the geographically adjacent Shiite minority of Saudi Arabia). If American influence could ever have turned an Arab country into a beacon of democracy, one might have expected that country to be Kuwait, for no Arab country so abjectly depends upon American protection. Regrettably, the al-Sabah dynasty that rules Kuwait has enshrined minority rule to an extent scarcely matched anywhere in the world, a fact that lends credibility, in the Muslim world, to the suspicion that the real U.S. interest is not democracy but oil.

Whatever the state of Kuwaiti civil rights, however, the United States has no moral right, even in retreat, to abandon a country that has been its military staging area for the unfinished American engagement in Iraq. Kuwait remains indispensable to the continued flow of Persian Gulf oil into the world economy and equally indispensable to the implementation of an orderly American withdrawal from Iraq.

West of Iraq, Syria, and Jordan are staggering under the impact of hundreds of thousands of Iraqi refugees—1.2 million in Syria (population 19 million) and a proportionately more burdensome 750,000 in Jordan (population only 6 million). The disruption occasioned by these refugee flows is not humanitarian alone, for some of the refugees bring with them the same sectarian rage that has cost so many lives in Iraq. Congress must mount a major humanitarian effort to assist these countries in coping with what promises to be a sharply increased flow of Iraqi refugees in the wake of the American withdrawal. Despite Syria's frozen relations with the United States, preserving its stability is more than a humanitarian duty: It is a tactical necessity if political meltdown in the region is to be avoided.

Southwest of Iraq, Saudi Arabia has built a multi-billion-dollar border fence against Iraqi refugees, but it shares an even longer, more lightly policed border with Jordan. Should Jordan become a failed state under the impact of massive Iraqi refugee flows and perhaps of civil war in Lebanon, al-Qaeda will undoubtedly use Jordan as ground zero for an all-out effort against Saudi Arabia, the birthplace of its own heretic-flogging Takfiri ideology and the greatest jihadi trophy of all. Congress should use that grim possibility to pressure Saudi Arabia to contribute more heavily to Iraqi refugee relief in the most affected countries, even if the Saudis continue to exclude Iraqi refugees themselves.

There remains to be said, finally, a word about the least mentionable item on the American agenda in Iraq—namely, Iraqi oil. Back in 1980, President Jimmy Carter—just months after the "crisis of confidence" speech in which he called for an all-out effort to break American dependence on Middle East oil—did not shrink from promising military action to protect "the Straits of Hormuz, a Persian Gulf waterway through which most of the world's oil must flow" and, within that action, to call for "the participation of all those who rely on oil from the Middle East." President George W. Bush, by contrast, during his tenure in office maintained a strange and studied silence about preserving the world's access to Persian Gulf oil.

In turning to this quintessentially un-religious topic, I mean to recall the peril mentioned near the start of this chapter—namely, the exaggeration of any single factor to the point that it excludes other relevant factors. Former Federal Reserve Chairman Alan Greenspan wrote in his 2008 memoir, *The Age of Turbulence,* "I am saddened that it is politically inconvenient to acknowledge what everyone knows: the Iraq war is largely about oil."[4] Many others are as saddened as he; for if there had been more honesty about American policy at the start, the United States would have had a wiser policy. In retrospect, the slogan of the many hundreds of thousands who demonstrated against the American invasion before it began, "No Blood for Oil," might more presciently have been "No Blood for No Oil," for the Bush administration would shed a great deal of American blood without procuring an inside track for American companies to the world's third- or second-largest proven petroleum reserve. The matter goes beyond anti-Americanism; non-American oil companies are properly daunted by the difficulties of drilling and refining in as traumatized and violence-prone a country as Iraq has become.

Even if Iraq remains too dangerous for foreign investment, Congress must at least take thought for preserving the world's access to the *rest* of the oil in the area: above all to Saudi oil. This is what makes peace with Iran so imperative; for even if the United States were to demolish Iran's nuclear installations, that country's naval and aerial capacity would still be sufficient to halt shipment through the Straits of Hormuz and to cripple oil production in Saudi Arabia. That such a blow would also strike Iran itself is less than reassuring. We are dealing, after all, with a regime whose religious calculus no one quite shares and no one can quite follow. Once again, we find ourselves at risk of projecting our own assumptions about what is reasonably, acceptably religious and what is fanatically, unacceptably religious upon a country that does not share those assumptions.

As the United States withdraws its forces from Iraq, it cannot afford to do as it did in Vietnam and leave its weaponry behind, for to do that would be to provide al-Qaeda an arsenal that it could use around the world. But if materiel as well as personnel is to be shipped out, then Congress must aim to stabilize the situation around Iraq long enough to buy the necessary time. Within war-shredded Iraq itself, Congress must salvage what remains of American honor, by expediting the immigration to this country of as many as possible of the Iraqis (with their families) who have risked so much to work with our forces in their homeland.

To envision withdrawal in even this much detail is, of course, to run well ahead of the American political debate in the last year or two of the second Bush administration, particularly as regarded the relevance of the deep religious divide in Iraq to the military victory that receded like a mirage whenever the American leadership declared it near. Even deep into his administration, former President Bush could not quite believe that the differences between Sunni and Shiites really mattered.

Shiite and Sunni combatants in the Iraq war may have shared a grim penchant for indiscriminate violence, but this was and is far from the only comment worth making about them. Former President Bush did American foreign policy no service when he fused them, declared them "totalitarian," as if to evoke the memory of the Soviet Union, and reduced their remaining differences to "different slogans." There is simply much more to it all than different slogans. Al-Qaeda, for example, a terrorist version of Sunni Islam, aspires to re-establish the caliphate, the long-abolished office of successor to Muhammad. But the caliphate was for centuries a symbol of Sunni oppression for Shiite Muslims, and one hears from that quarter no calls for its restoration. This and other differences present different openings for negotiation and might even dictate distinctly different military tactics.

Official American determination to gloss over religious differences among our enemies in Iraq, lest we seem to be enmeshed in a civil war, has mirrored the mentioned U.S. determination to minimize the corresponding differences among our friends, lest the task of nation-building emerge in its true complexity. Thus, in a typical statement, U.S. Ambassador to Iraq Ryan Crocker and Army Gen. David H. Petraeus characterized the horrendous July 9, 2007, massacre of Iraqi Turkmens as "another sad example of the nature of the enemy." The sadness of the example is beyond dispute, but "*the* enemy," whenever "he" is spoken of that way, is an artificial, unitized terrorist Iraqi whose peaceful civilian counterpart is that purple-fingered patriot whom President Bush made to stand for the supposed plain-Iraqi majority of the Iraqi population. The unitized, secularized, and misrepresented enemy is thus made to match the unitized, secularized, and equally misrepresented friend.

This is the kind of thinking that, for so long, blinded American policymakers to the deep mutual hostility between the Soviet Union and the People's Republic of China and prevented the separate approach to each that helped end the Cold War.

For too long, the two were unitized as a single great communist enemy, and any differences between them were mere differences of slogan. In an only somewhat smaller theater, this is the kind of thinking that led policymakers to believe that in fighting Vietnamese communism, they were fighting the imperial designs of Chinese communism when, again, the two nations were mutually suspicious and would later become actively hostile. Russia was a historically expansionist power; China was not. Fifty thousand Americans died because of the delusion that Communist China aspired to devour Vietnam as Soviet Russia had devoured the Baltic states.

The differences between Russian and Chinese communism were ideological and cultural rather than, in the usual sense, religious. The differences between Sunni and Shiite Islam, though also ideological and cultural, are crucially religious; and their consequences are large. Vali Nasr, in *The Shia Revival: How Conflicts Within Islam Will Shape the Future,* sees the Iran-Iraq war as a religious proxy war in which Saudi Arabia and Kuwait funded the Iraqi side as a way of chastening the specifically religious ambitions of Ayatollah Khomeini and the Islamic Revolution to replace the Saudis as guardians and custodians of Mecca and Medina. The deposed Shah Reza Pahlavi, with no such ambitions, had never attracted such concerted Sunni or Arabian hostility.

At the peak of Sunni-sponsored terrorism in Iraq, according to official U.S. military sources, 45% of the "foreign fighters" and "foreign facilitators" fighting alongside al-Qaeda-in-Mesopotamia were Saudis, proxy warriors for the Sunni side in the Iraq civil war. That some Iraqi Sunnis eventually withdrew their welcome from this kind of Saudi "help" does not strip the cross-border flow of all continuing relevance. King Abdullah of Saudi Arabia has shown transparent hostility toward Iraq's Shiite prime minister as well as to the American intervention in Iraq itself, which Saudi Arabia (like every nation in the region except Kuwait and Israel) opposed from the outset. The Saudi volunteers in Iraq may be unofficially implementing the Wahhabi intentions of their king or of other powerful Arabian interests.

The United States, having already taken casualties on both sides of the Iraq civil war, has no intention of taking on the suppliers of both sides—that is, both Saudi Arabia and Iran. As the religious dimension of the war comes into retrospective focus, however, this potential regionalization of it—not after but through the American intervention—comes into focus as well. By the standards of religious war, one recalls, a ten-year war must count as extremely short.

The exit strategy that has been devised must develop into a regional, religiously informed policy if its effect is not to bring about repetition on a larger scale. A religiously informed regional policy need not entail any formal American engagement with the Sunni/Shiite religious difference. Nonetheless, religious insight of a sort—acknowledgment, namely, that the civil war that has been under way has been genuinely and not just apparently religious and that it could spread beyond Iraq—is among the conditions for an informed and reasonably durable policy.

As the United States gradually exits Iraq, the eyes and ears of the Muslim world are trained on the incumbent American president as never before in our history. President Obama has seized this moment twice — briefly in his address to the Turkish parliament and more programmatically in his June 2009 address at Al-Azhaar University in Cairo. The Cairo address was historic in that never before had an American president addressed himself at such length to *any* religion's adherents. And yet much more remains to be said, and a long list of capitals in Muslim-majority capitals would welcome a presidential visit during which the President might say, and then say again, and then repeat:

- that though the United States has a national way of dealing with religion; we have no national religion;

- that our national way of dealing with religion allows full scope for the free practice of Islam within our borders;

- that ours is a country in which a Muslim could someday be elected president — or a Jew or a Hindu or a Buddhist;

- that when we go to war, we do not go to war in the name of Christianity, despite the fact that a majority of our citizens are Christians;

- that whatever mistakes were made in our attempt to overthrow Saddam Hussein and give Iraq back to the Iraqis, it is not now and never has been a part of our agenda to deter anyone from the practice of Islam;

- and, finally, that where violent rivalries arise among Muslims, while we regret them as much as we regret violence among Christians or Hindus or any other believers, we cannot regard the resolution of such conflicts as properly our responsibility; the trauma of *fitna* carried to murderous, Takfiri extremes is a wound that Muslims themselves, not outsiders, must heal.

All this desperately needs to be said, and a better time to say it may never come. The greatest of the long-term lessons to be learned from the historic blunder of the second Gulf War must be never again to underestimate the soft power of religious difference to trump the supposedly hard realities of guns and money. Whether the American people themselves learn this lesson or not will depend in the short run on what they hear from their leadership as the war ends, but in the long run it will depend on what it learns from its news media. It matters therefore what lessons the press will draw from this debacle.

The press will have learned from the second Gulf War if future coverage of this region reflects a deeper understanding of the relevance of religion to its divisions and to its various cultural identities. The war has exposed some of the internal complexity of Iraq. One would welcome coverage reflecting comparable sensitivity to the distinct differences, where religion is concerned, that obtain within Iran and sometimes bind regions of that country to cross-border regions of other countries or to other entire nations.

The Azeris of northwestern Iran, for example, share language and, to a considerable extent, culture with Azerbaijan, but Azerbaijan established a secular political culture even earlier than Turkey did under Kemal Atatürk early in the twentieth century. Turkey and Azerbaijan are, in their cultural similarity and the size of their populations, analogous to Germany and Austria or the United States and Canada. The Turkish and the Azeri languages are closely related and, to a point, mutually intelligible. But the Turks are overwhelmingly Sunni, and the Azeris almost as overwhelmingly Shiite. And there is a further religious complication: Azerbaijan has been locked in a territorial war with post-Soviet Armenia for many years. Yet Turkey and Christian Armenia seem now ready to make peace, and Azerbaijan and Christian Georgia are already cooperating closely. Do these developments have any implications for Iran?

The economic rationale for the mentioned rapprochements is powerful and powerfully oil-related, yet its religious implications could be significant as well—even as far away as Iran. I offer no more than an example of the kind of alertness to religion that might enable a foreign correspondent, television producer, or editorial commentator to do a better job in reporting on these areas, which could explode into front-page and prime-time news at any moment.

The news media may properly take pride in the extent to which they are reviled for never getting anything right. Their myriad critics betray the high hopes they still entertain for journalism and their dependence upon it. Its only duty is to the truth, the truth pure and simple; but as Oscar Wilde wryly put it, the truth is rarely pure and never simple. To plead for its inclusion in a journalist's mental checklist or working heuristic is to plead for no more than the truth in all its impure unsimplicity.

SUGGESTED DISCUSSION QUESTIONS

1. The author begins by taking note of journalism's traditional five W's: Who, What, When, Where, Why. He suggests that the "Why" has become ever more significant in print news stories, and that the "Who, What, When, and Where" have become less significant than they ought to be in other forms of media. What inferences can be drawn from this observation about the depth and quality of current reporting on complicated international stories like Iraq?

2. What are the most important religious and ethnic conflicts within Iraq and what are the complicating factors for journalists in trying to understand them?

3. What advice does the author have early in the chapter for journalists when assessing international events, and why do you think they so often are caught having missed important considerations in their coverage?

4. Coverage of the conflicts in Iraq and the Mideast often begin with secular considerations. Does this approach interfere with the reportage on events past and present in Iraq?

5. The author talks about "a norm for attainable excellence" for journalists in approaching a foreign conflict that is new to them. What does he think journalists can and should be expected to do?

6. What was the critical religious element missed by the news media in the very beginning of the Iraq War, information that should have been available to inform reporters' ability to ask good questions?

7. The author writes, "The responsible journalist must begin from the premise that the relationship of civil and religious elements differs from any one society to the next, (and) that most complex social arrangements have latent functions that an outsider is particularly likely to miss . . ." Discuss.

8. The author says that in the Muslim world suspicion that "the real U.S. interest is not democracy but oil" is credible due to the political situation in Kuwait. Discuss this point.

9. Studies by the Project for Excellence in Journalism have revealed that the American public no longer trusts the press to be a force in favor of democracy. Perhaps one way to change this perception is to ensure that the press covers U.S. foreign policy with the nuance it deserves. Cite examples given in this chapter that illustrate the point.

10. Journalism performs a public service by monitoring the powerful and by explaining complicated underlying factors in the news. How does an understanding of religious forces in the news factor into these roles of reporters?

ENDNOTES

1. *The Columbia Encyclopedia,* 6th ed., s.v. "Paris, in Greek Mythology."

2. Christopher Marlowe, *The Tragical History of Dr. Faustus,* ed. F. J. Cox, London: Francis Griffiths, 1907, p. 66.

3. http://www.youtube.com/watch?v=6BEsZMvrq-I&feature=relatedIn.

4. Jack Miles, "The Sovereignty Showdown in Iraq" for TomDispatch.com, October 24, 2007.

CHAPTER 4

Religion and National Politics

Benjamin J. Hubbard

The author is Professor Emeritus of Comparative Religion, California State University, Fullerton, and for many years has taught journalism and communications students in his popular course, "Religion and Media." He is an expert on the evolution of religion coverage in the press. Here he recounts some of that history, and brings readers up to date with a discussion of the 2008 presidential campaign.

PART I: A SYNOPSIS OF RELIGION REPORTING OVER THE PAST HALF CENTURY

Twenty years ago, I wrote a chapter, "The Importance of the Religion Angle in Reporting on Current Events" in *Reporting Religion — Facts and Faith*.[1] That angle is even more important now than it was then. This essay will trace the evolution of religion reporting in the secular press, summarize key studies of this press specialty, review some of the memorable religion-in-politics moments of past decades and focus on an analysis of religion coverage in the 2008 presidential campaign and its implications for today's reporters.

The Evolution of Religion Reporting

The "church pages" of another era consisted mainly of sermon summaries, announcements, and other parochial matters. But when the Associated Press appointed George Cornell to a religion specialty desk in 1951, the situation changed. Cornell possessed a brilliant ability to see and report the religion angle in national and world affairs, and many papers began running his stories. At around the same time, in 1949, the Religion Newswriters Association was formed in an effort to further profession-alize the field. Between then and 1988 it grew from 33 members to 288. That number held fairly steady until about six years ago when the demise of so many dailies began to affect layoffs — with religion writers often among the first to go.[2] (More about this later.)

Along with the AP's Cornell, a second-generation religion writer, John Dart, for-merly of the *Los Angeles Times,* was very influential both as a reporter and a mentor for others in the field. Dart covered religion from 1967 to 1998 and was especially in-fluential in making the public aware of the latest developments in biblical scholar-ship. Dart also wrote two guides for religion writers, *Deities & Deadlines* (2nd ed., 1998) and *Bridging the Gap — Religion and the News Media* (2000). The former is more a handbook of key facts and terms about religious groups, while the latter — co-written with Dr. Jimmy Allen, a former president of the Southern Baptist Convention — is a valuable discussion of the whole field of religion coverage, includ-ing a comprehensive survey (see below).

Additionally, Kenneth Woodward, religion editor at *Newsweek* for 38 years, was a pioneer religion writer. Woodward started covering the subject around the time of the Second Vatican Council. His work was highly informative on issues ranging from the civil rights movement, to Billy Graham's influence on Richard Nixon, and of course to Vatican II. Woodward wrote some 750 articles for the magazine, including 100 cover stories.

The growth in religion reporting was helped significantly by momentous events involving religion and religious leaders: the rebirth of a Jewish Commonwealth, the State of Israel, after 1,900 years; the formation of the World Council of Churches in 1949; the Second Vatican Council (1962–1965); and the civil rights and anti-war move-ments of the 1960s and early 1970s in which religious figures — most notably the Rev. Martin Luther King, Jr. — were involved.

Next came the 1973 Roe v. Wade Supreme Court decision about abortion, and the powerful reaction by evangelical Christians. After decades of staying out of the po-litical arena, conservative Christians mobilized for action under the pro-life aegis of the Rev. Jerry Falwell's Moral Majority, Pat Robertson's Christian Coalition, Dr. James Dobson's Focus on the Family, the Operation Rescue movement led by Randall Terry, and the unified stand of the country's Roman Catholic bishops, especially Joseph Car-dinal Bernardin of Chicago, with his consistent life ethic (opposition to abortion, cap-ital punishment, and war).

Evangelicals took up two other causes in the final decades of the 20th century: opposition to the gay rights movement and to the teaching of evolution in public schools. These conflicts pitted conservative Christians and Jews against their liberal counterparts who were pro-choice, open to the gay rights movement, and solidly op-posed to the creationism and intelligent design theories which tried to refute evolution. So there has been plenty of religious controversy in the 37 years since abortion was legalized, and journalism loves a good fight. Not all of the coverage was sufficiently in-depth, but it was reasonably comprehensive.

Then there were the scandals: Jim and Tammy Faye Bakker's misappropriation of funds for a Christian theme park and resort that led to a criminal conviction against Jim; the Rev. Jimmy Swaggert's liaison with a prostitute followed by his lugubrious TV confession; the admission by the Rev. Ted Haggard, then-president of the National Association of Evangelicals, of his sexual relationship with a male masseur; and the pedophilia scandal among Roman Catholic clergy that led to the resignation of Bernard Cardinal Law of Boston, several criminal convictions and the payout of over a billion dollars to hundreds of victims. In the Bakker and priestly sex abuse cases, there were Pulitzer Prizes for the investigative reporters of the *Charlotte Observer* and *Boston Globe* respectively. And in both cases the papers were accused (by Jim Bakker and Cardinal Law) of biased coverage.

Along with these contentious religious issues in the United States and Canada, the Islamic revolution in Iran under Ayatollah Ruhollah Khomeini in 1978 made the western world take note of the rise of radical Islam. In the early stages of the revolution, journalistic understanding of Islam was deficient. Gradually over the next 30 years it has significantly improved, as Phil Bennett's chapter in this volume illustrates.

Finally, the religious views of former presidents, especially Jimmy Carter, have been the focus of religion reporting—not all of it enlightening. In Carter's case, the press was fascinated with his unashamed declaration that he was a born-again Christian. However, it failed to factor his faith into his political worldview, leading Carter to remark that, "The press had no desire to explain my faith or understand it." Thus, when the former president succeeded in convincing Israeli Prime Minister Menachem Begin and Egyptian President Anwar Sadat to sign their 1979 peace treaty, the religious motivations prompting Carter to push for the treaty—his conviction that the three shared a common Abrahamic monotheism—received too little coverage.

Similarly, President Ronald Reagan's fascination with Armageddon and the end times during his first term, and its connection to his policy toward the Soviet Union was overlooked by political reporters.[3]

Public Demand for More Comprehensive Religion Reporting

Along with the increase in both the quality and frequency of religion stories in the past half century, public demand was another factor contributing to growth in good reporting. For instance, the Lilly Endowment sponsored a nationwide study in 1988–1989, *The RNS-Lily Study of Religion Reporting and Readership in the Daily Press*. It consisted of a random national sample of 1,100 adults, and in-depth interviews with clerical and lay leaders at six churches and with 16 religion writers. The study concluded that:

1. Readers want more serious religion news rather than soft items about church social events and the like. They also expect the same level of professionalism in religion stories as in other news.
2. There are many religiously observant people who nevertheless do not read denominational papers or magazines and, consequently, need their daily paper to provide religion coverage.
3. Religion news was neither the most nor least important kind of news they expected from their papers, but came somewhere in between.
4. Readers were generally dissatisfied with the quality of religion news.
5. Both readers and editors want to see religion news mainstreamed, not confined to a religion page (and, the study notes, this was already happening in the late 1980s).
6. Journalists and editors are more comfortable when religion stories are covered in the same manner as news about politics, business, scandals, and health.

In the winter of 1992–1993, the First Amendment Center affiliated with Vanderbilt University did a comprehensive survey of Protestant and Catholic clergy, newspaper editors and religion writers on whether news coverage is biased against religion. Its findings:

1. The clergy thought religion reporting was "too sensational" and should include more spiritually uplifting stories. The writers disagreed sharply with the first point but had some appreciation for the second.
2. Nearly 80 percent of the journalists thought the public has benefitted from stories about corrupt evangelists, pedophiliac priests, and dangerous sects. The clergy were less convinced: liberal Protestants agreed 5 to 3, Catholics were evenly split, and evangelicals disagreed 5 to 3.
3. Almost 60 percent of the clergy thought the writers should be religiously active, but only 20 percent of them agreed.
4. Yet, three-quarters of the journalists surveyed said faith was "very important" in their lives. Among the editors, 35 percent saw religion as "very important" in their lives and 37 percent "somewhat important."

Thus, there was some disagreement in the survey between clergy and media professionals about the quality of religion coverage but certainly not a consensus that the media were trying to tear down faith.

Then in 1999, the Garrett-Medill Center for Religion and the News Media at Northwestern University, with funding from the Ford Foundation, produced *Media Coverage of Religion, Spirituality and Values*. It was a content analysis based on a sampling of news from nationally prominent print and television media during 28 randomly sampled days by a team of researchers. In all, they reviewed 2,350 print and electronic stories on all topics. Their principal findings were:

1.   Between 11 and 14 percent of all these stories were about religion, spirituality, or values; most were fairly prominent; and a few were top news stories.
2.   Most of the stories were about organized religion, with a fair number about spirituality but only a few about values. Between 14 and 25 percent of the stories featured religion or spirituality as the primary element.
3.   Religion-related stories focused mainly on the monotheistic faiths, with Christianity getting the most coverage, followed by Judaism and then Islam. Other faiths received only scant coverage. Islam was mentioned in only 1 percent of TV reports, 8 percent of newspaper articles, and 12 percent of magazine stories. (I am sure a similar study today would find many more stories about Islam.)
4.   Articles on religion, spirituality, and values portrayed religious traditions and key terms without bias but also without much context.

Yet another study of religion reporting, *Media Coverage of Religion in America: 1969–1998,* appeared in 2000. It resembled the Garrett-Medill endeavor by being a content analysis of almost the same set of media outlets, but it covered a longer time period and had a more political focus as seen in its conclusions:

1.   Religion's role in politics and in conflicts involving church governance were two of the most covered topics.
2.   Theological or spiritual issues were seldom presented as newsworthy either in themselves or in relation to larger social issues. Even when religious groups provided input to public policy debates, the theological rationales for a particular faith's position were usually overlooked by the press.
3.   On questions of sexual morality (abortion, homosexuality, etc.), editorial opinion tended to reaffirm conservative positions. The only exception involved the Catholic Church's stand on artificial contraception.
4.   However, on issues involving progressive politics (e.g., the role of women and minorities in religious institutions and a greater role for the laity in church governance), the media studied took more liberal positions.
5.   There was a significant increase, during the 30-year period studied, in coverage of criminal and other forms of misconduct by clergy, especially Roman Catholic priests. (Sad to say, more priestly criminality was just on the horizon.)
6.   The period from 1988–1998 revealed increased attention, and more diverse perspectives, to religion-related news. Journalists covered more faiths and more issues.
7.   Finally, one reason for this increased attention may be that reporters were becoming more attuned to the sphere of faith. In 1980, for example, 50 percent of them had no religious affiliation, while in 1995 the percentage of the nonaffiliated had dropped to 22 percent.

Finally, in May 2007, Media Matters for America[4] released *Left Behind: The Skewed Representation of Religion in Major News Media*. It focused on a very specific issue: how often conservative and progressive religious leaders are interviewed, quoted, or mentioned in news stories. The study found:

1. In all media, print and electronic, conservative religious leaders were interviewed, quoted, or mentioned 2.8 times as often as progressive leaders.
2. On national TV news networks, conservatives received 3.8 times as much coverage.
3. This skewing of coverage toward conservatives "represents a particularly meaningful distortion," because progressive religious leaders often focus on different issues and provide distinct perspectives (for example, gay rights, abortion, and stem-cell research).

In summary, these studies indicate that, over the past half-century, readers have asked for and gotten more and better religion news, and that this news has gradually been more often mainstreamed, rather than confined to a church page. However, the studies also indicated that stories about religion's role in politics and conflict tended to predominate, that the underlying religious or theological convictions behind a story seldom received attention, and that the views of conservative religious authorities tended to get more press than their liberal counterparts. Also, according to the First Amendment Center survey, clergy tend to believe that religion news is too sensational and to some extent too critical.

Religion Reporting Comes to Television

As the new millennium began, the long drought of in-depth religion reporting on television ended. *Religion and Ethics Newsweekly* debuted on PBS[5] under the superb leadership of the veteran NBC-TV journalist Bob Abernethy. This weekly 30-minute program has significantly increased the availability of unbiased news about religious and ethical issues to the American public and to schools and universities.

Through its *Frontline* and other series, PBS has also produced several fine religion-oriented programs over many years, such as the multi-part investigations of the Church of Jesus Christ of Latter-day Saints in "The Mormons" and of Judaism in "The Jewish Americans." Moreover, both CNN and the History Channel began producing in-depth specials on religion topics in the past decade. CNN'S "The Mystery of Jesus" (2004), for example, was balanced and informative.

Weekly newsmagazines also have produced a significantly greater number of cover stories about religious movements or personalities in the past decade. For example, Pope John Paul II, the Dalai Lama, and Billy Graham have been on the covers of *Time* and *Newsweek,* and *US News* produced a special collector's edition, "Secrets of

Islam (The Essential Guide to the World's Fastest Growing Religion)" in 2005. Among monthly periodicals, the *Atlantic Monthly* has consistently covered religion with in-depth pieces. In March 2008, for instance, the magazine's cover headline was "Which Religion Will Win," and featured three essays that dealt with the new, more moderate evangelicals; the Christian-Muslim contest for souls in Nigeria; and the prospects for inter-religious peace in a more secularized world. In addition, Lisa Miller — religion editor at *Newsweek* since 2006 — has written several significant essays, such as "The Politics of Jesus" (Oct. 13, 2006) which examined the impact of faith in the mid-term congressional elections.

One specialized, first-rate periodical deserves mention: *Religion in the News,* produced for the past 12 years by the Center for the Study of Religion in Public Life at Trinity College in Hartford. The winter 2008 issue included a piece about the religiosity of all of the then-Republican presidential candidates, as well as specific articles about the religious roots of Gov. Mike Huckabee and Gov. Mitt Romney. Most of its work over the years, however, has focused on how well the secular press has handled a particular story, e.g., the priestly pedophilia scandal, the uproar over the Danish cartoons about Prophet Muhammad, or the damage done to Jewish philanthropic institutions by the Ponzi schemes of Bernard Madoff.

PART II: RELIGION COVERAGE OF THE 2008 PRESIDENTIAL CONTEST

Amid the ongoing struggles of daily newspapers to survive, as already noted, a number of fine religion writers either have lost their jobs or been reassigned. Hence, it is more and more often becoming the responsibility of general assignment reporters to cover the religious dimensions of the news, especially as it intersects with politics. This was certainly true of Election 2008 on which we now focus.

Although the 1960 presidential race brought John F. Kennedy's Catholicism to the fore, and the 1976 contest Jimmy Carter's "born-again" background, no race in memory has had a "religion angle" as conspicuous as in 2008. The Pew Forum compiled an exhaustive content analysis of the election, *How the News Media Covered Religion in the General Election*[6] which illustrates powerfully the extent to which religion factored into politics. Among the study's key findings:

1. Press accounts related to religion comprised 4 percent of the general election's "news hole," the total space or time available in a media outlet for news content. This was less than news of the economic crisis (9 percent) or Iraq (6 percent) but equal to coverage of the Republican National Convention and greater than news of energy issues (2 percent) or the environment (>1 percent).
2. Religion storylines in which candidate Obama was the lead newsmaker comprised 53 percent of all coverage of the presidential and vice-presidential candidates. Most of these stories involved controversy or had an unfavorable cast.

The majority of the Obama-focused stories dealt with rumors that he was a Muslim, followed by his association with controversial pastor Jeremiah Wright, Jr. By contrast, John McCain was the focus of just 9 percent of religion-related coverage, and his running mate Sarah Palin, 19 percent. Most of the Palin coverage involved family or personal issues (especially her teenage daughter's pregnancy). Stories about Joe Biden were scarce (0.7 percent).

3. All four of the candidates had pastor problems of some sort—most notably Obama's with Rev. Wright, followed by McCain's with Pastor John Hagee.
4. The Saddleback Civil Forum on the Presidency, moderated by Pastor Rick Warren at his huge church in Lake Forest, CA, on August 16, 2008, garnered brief but intense coverage that amounted to 10 percent of total news in the week of the event but quickly faded.[7]
5. Ethical issues involving religion and culture comprised less than 1 percent of total campaign news—most of it tied to Palin's views on abortion.

Next, we turn to specifics—the subject matter and quality of religion-related stories about the four presidential candidates along with a brief discussion of the coverage of one candidate from the Republican presidential primary, Mitt Romney. His case is important for an understanding of how the "religion angle" should be handled.

Barack Obama and His Outspoken Pastor

As noted, the controversial sermons of Barack Obama's former pastor at Trinity United Church of Christ in Chicago, Dr. Jeremiah Wright, Jr., and their fallout on the Obama presidential campaign were an important news focus. In fact, they accounted for 9 percent of all religion-related campaign stories. Some of Wright's comments—taken in the raw without any context—were very controversial and distressed many people, including Obama. To say, "The chickens have come to roost" (shades of Malcolm X's comment after President Kennedy's assassination) following September 11, 2001 is hardly endearing to the general public. And "God damn America" made even political lefties cringe. Those comments, however, were not uttered in isolation but in the midst of highly emotional sermons about racial injustice, America's sometimes controversial foreign policy, and the plight of some of Wright's South Side Chicago congregants struggling with unemployment and poverty.

Ironically, the former Republican presidential candidate Mike Huckabee, a former preacher himself, might have provided the most insightful comment on the controversy: "There are things that sometimes get said [in sermons] that, if you put them on paper and looked at them in print, you'd say, 'Well, I didn't mean to say it quite like that.'"

In any case, once excerpts from Wright's fiery sermons hit YouTube, the conservative "commentariate"—Rush Limbaugh, Sean Hannity, Bill O'Reilly, et al.—began to pillory Obama without mercy (or context). To its credit, many centrist and liberal newspapers and magazines tried to contextually situate Wright's blunt rhetoric. Stuart Silverstein of the *Los Angeles Times* (March 19, 2008), for example, noted the very positive overall thrust of Wright's preaching philosophy — to uplift and inspire. Thus, Wright told members of LA's Church of God in Christ several years ago, "Don't give up on God! . . . Don't give up on the process of marriage." Silverstein also noted Wright's six years of military service between 1964 and 1970. Lisa Miller of *Newsweek* (March 24, 2008) also provided a balanced, insightful analysis of the controversy, noting the extraordinarily good work of Trinity United in its AIDS ministry, assistance to senior citizens, etc.

But Obama had to respond fully to his pastor's disturbing words (which he had already disavowed in one of the presidential primary debates). He did so in a powerful speech in Philadelphia on March 18. Obama unequivocally condemned Wright's inflammatory rhetoric, saying that his words, ". . . expressed a profoundly distorted view of this country . . . that elevates what is wrong with America above all that we know is right with America." But he also lauded his former pastor for his social justice ministry. Obama spoke candidly of the anger still simmering in Black America, yet also noted the struggles of working class whites. And he observed that the African-American community needed to "embrace the burden of our past without becoming victims of our present."

The *New York Times* editorialized on March 19, 2008 that Obama, ". . . drew a bright line between his religious connection with Mr. Wright, which should be none of the voters' business, and having a political connection, which should be very much their business. The distinction seems especially urgent after seven years of a president who has worked to blur the line between church and state." Steven Greenhut, writing in the conservative-libertarian *Orange County Register* on March 22, 2008, opined that the Obama speech sounded surprisingly conservative at points, for example, his comment that economic problems in the Black community had resulted both from "the legacy of legalized discrimination, but also from 'the erosion of black families' and failed welfare policies." Greenhut also mentioned the endorsement of Sen. John McCain's candidacy by the fundamentalist pastor John Hagee, whose anti-Catholic rhetoric was very troubling to many.

Writing in the *Columbia Journalism Review's* online blog March 14, 2008, Zachary Roth noted McCain's calling the mega-church pastor Rod Parsely "a spiritual guide." Parsely has called on Christians to wage war against the "false religion of Islam" to destroy it and makes no distinction between Muslim extremists and moderates. Yet, Roth couldn't find one mainstream U.S. news outlet that even mentioned McCain's connection to this extremist pastor.

Later in the campaign, Obama severed relations with Wright and resigned from Trinity United after the pastor made a number of inflammatory statements during an appearance at the National Press Club.

In summary, the Obama-Wright controversy is an example of the importance of contextualization, balance, and historical memory[8] in reporting on political controversies, especially when there is a religious dimension to the story.

McCain's Pastor Problems

Though not as serious as Obama's affiliation with Rev. Wright, candidate McCain also got a lesson in the perils of connections to outspoken pastors.

Rev. Hagee, leader of an evangelical mega-church in San Antonio, Texas, endorsed him early in the campaign. However, Hagee, who later apologized, had said Adolph Hitler's anti-Semitism was a fulfillment of God's will because it would hasten the Jews' return to Israel in accord with his reading of biblical prophecy. (Hagee had also disparaged Catholicism in some of his sermons.) When McCain learned of these comments, he quickly distanced himself from the pastor and the issue faded. A backgrounder on why some evangelical ministers are prone to such bizarre interpretations of the Bible would have been useful, but nothing surfaced in the mainstream press.

Obama, the 'Clandestine Muslim'

Rumors that President Obama was a Muslim accounted for 30 percent of all religion-related campaign news in the Pew survey. Two other surveys by the Pew Research Center (in June 2008 and October 2008) both found that 12 percent of the electorate believed the rumor. Obama's Kenyan father was born Muslim but had become a non-believer; and his stepfather, Lolo Soetoro, was a non-practicing Muslim. Moreover, from age eight to ten, the President while in Indonesia attended a private elementary school—though not a Muslim madrassa—that had a largely Muslim student body. However, he never converted to Islam, and at ten was sent by his mother, also a non-religious person, to live with her parents in Hawaii.

A June 21, 2008 *New Yorker* magazine cover depicted Barack in typical Muslim dress and his wife Michelle as a Black Power radical—shades of 1960s professor and activist Angela Davis. Though the cover and the magazine's accompanying story, "The Politics of Fear," were intended to dispel the Muslim rumor, they kept the story alive. In fact, the Obama team, even before the *New Yorker* story appeared, had set up a website, www.fightthesmears.com, to stem the rumors.

Conservative commentators Limbaugh and Hannity criticized the Obama camp over an incident, also in June, when his staffers removed from camera view two women wearing Muslim head scarves during a campaign rally. Appearing on NBC's *Meet the Press,* (October 19, 2008) former Secretary of State Colin Powell, noting that Obama was, in fact, Christian, got to the heart of the controversy. He asked, "What if he is [Muslim]? Is there something wrong with being a Muslim in this country? The answer's no. That's not America. Is something wrong with a seven-year-old Muslim-American kid believing that he or she could be president?"

Writing in *The Miami Herald* on June 29, Leonard Pitts, Jr., observed that candidate Obama had apologized for the flap with the Muslim women. But he said the apology would have seemed more sincere if Obama had been courageous enough to point there is nothing wrong with being an American Muslim (`a la Powell) and "... hadn't spent so much time treating the American Muslim community as one does the carrier of a contagious disease."[9] Pitts does grant that candidate Obama was walking "an unprecedented political tightrope, one part John F. Kennedy, one part Jackie Robinson." Still, Pitts felt the candidate's "standoffishness" toward American Muslims was a mistake.

In sum, with few exceptions, the press failed to sufficiently investigate the roots of anti-Muslim sentiment in America and make clear, as Powell and Pitts did, that there is no "religious test" for public office in this country, in accord with Article VI of the Constitution.

The Personal Faith of the Presidential Candidates

Barack Obama

A June 21, 2008 *Newsweek* essay by Lisa Miller and Richard Wolffe, "Finding His Faith," was a fine exposition of Obama's faith journey. It was accompanied by a sidebar from the magazine's editor, Jon Meacham, which—like the Miller-Wolffe piece—exhibited a high degree of religious literacy. Meacham discussed the influence of the Founding Fathers, Abraham Lincoln and Reinhold Niebuhr on Obama's theological world view. Meacham quoted the then-candidate on the necessity of having a "north star" of faith to guide a president, as it had guided Lincoln during the dark night of the Civil War.

The principal locale for a discussion of Obama's and McCain's faith was Rick Warren's Civil Forum mentioned above in connection with the Pew survey. Though the abortion debate accounted for only 5 percent of the forum's content, it received most of the coverage in mainstream media. By contrast almost 20 percent of the forum dealt with the candidates' religious beliefs but received scant notice. Yet, the candidates discussed significant religious and ethical questions: the moral obligation to provide for "the least of these" (Obama, alluding to the Gospel of Matthew 25:45), the fortifying power of faith, personal moral failures, etc. As in the case of Jimmy Carter's personal faith more than 30 years ago, the press largely failed to analyze the implications of the candidates' religious views for how they would govern. It is important for political reporters to distinguish between (a) using a politician's religious affiliation (Catholic, evangelical, Mormon, Muslim, etc.) to question his ability to govern fairly— almost always a mistake; and (b) analyzing his or her core moral positions to determine how these might affect a president's decisions—a benefit.

John McCain

Turning to coverage of McCain's faith, one notes far less content, mainly because the Arizona senator said less about it and didn't have the significant pastor problems that Obama did. McCain occasionally spoke of how faith helped him survive captivity at the hands of the North Vietnamese, as he did in an August 18, 2008 *Time* magazine interview. In the Saddleback forum, he expressed his theology in a single sentence: "I'm saved and I'm forgiven." Regarding his core moral positions, whose importance to good reporting was just mentioned, Michael Gerson, wrote perceptively about him in a *Newsweek* essay on September 8, 2008. He pointed out that McCain might be reticent to speak about his faith, but his moral positions as a senator—opposing torture, recognizing the humanity of undocumented immigrants, condemning the slaughter in Darfur—manifest "a code, combining a religious concern for the weak and the oppressed with a military conception of national honor . . ." And Mecham was eloquent in interviews on National Public Radio on October 29 and 30, 2008, when he observed that both Obama and McCain believed in doing the right, and both saw the world as tragic, yet knew they must do their best to improve or heal it.

Sarah Palin

Candidate Palin's family and personal issues comprised about a quarter of all the religion-related campaign stories, but most involved the pregnancy of her unwed daughter and her opposition to abortion and stem-cell research. A 2005 video of the Kenyan Pentecostal preacher Thomas Muthee laying hands on Palin at the Wasilla Assembly of God Church while she was running for governor of Alaska caused a brief media stir during the presidential race. Two weeks before being tapped by McCain as his running mate, Palin was asked about her religious affiliation. "Christian," she replied; asked whether she was a particular kind, she responded, "No. Bible-believing."[10] She had, though, attended the Wasilla Assembly for a number of years. Harking back to Colin Powell's retort about whether there was anything wrong about a Muslim being president, how about being a Pentecostal?

In a valuable background piece on Palin, Teresa Watanabe of the *Los Angeles Times* (October 1, 2008) reported on the candidate's decision to accept the vice-presidential nomination in light of her evangelical, Bible-centered faith. Three New Testament letters (Ephesians, 1 Timothy, and Titus) state that a woman's place is in the home and she should be obedient to her husband. Watanabe found a difference of opinion among evangelical leaders. Some were dismayed by Palin's decision, others approved as long as her husband concurred and it was understood that a woman could direct a nation or state but not a religious congregation.

Joe Biden

Biden's Roman Catholic faith generated scant news during the campaign except in connection with his pro-choice stance. On NBC'S *Meet the Press* on September 7, 2008, Tom Brokaw asked him what he'd say if asked by Obama when life begins. Biden replied that he knew when it began according to his Catholic faith (at conception), but added, ". . . for me to impose that judgment on others is inappropriate in a pluralistic society." As in the case of the 2004 presidential candidate John Kerry—also a pro-choice Catholic—several bishops were critical of Biden, but the abortion issue faded both for Biden and for the electorate in general.

Mitt Romney

Though former Massachusetts governor Mitt Romney lost the Republican primary, press (and public) scrutiny, and suspicion about his Mormon faith deserves comment. Because the LDS church allowed polygamy until 1890, kept African-Americans from the priestly rank until 1976, and is viewed as a cult by some conservative Christians, Romney began his campaign with particular liabilities. Michael Kinsley, writing in *Time* on September 17, 2007, wanted to know how candidates would deal with "religion's improbabilities." And he was especially concerned with those faith dimensions in the Mormon tradition. However, all religions rest on improbabilities. So it is important for journalists to temper their skepticism and realize that competent politicians are able to separate matters of state from matters of the spirit. President Kennedy didn't take orders from the pope, despite the fears of some Protestants in 1960. Romney would not have taken his from the Mormon president. This doesn't mean that a candidate's religious and ethical convictions should not be factored onto one's voting decisions, but rather that his or her political views and record are of much greater importance.[11]

Final Observations on the Candidates' Faith

The unprecedented amount of God talk in the 2008 campaign—and the precarious pastor connections discussed here—led Peter Canellos of the *Boston Globe* to observe that, in seeking to inject some religion into their campaigns, the candidates learned that religion and politics is a difficult mix.[12] On the whole question of a presidential candidate's faith, Nancy Gibbs, in a June 30, 2008, *Time* essay, wrote perceptively that Americans have always said in surveys that they want a person of faith in the White House. However, this time around the bar was set so high that pastor connections nearly capsized Obama's election ship and didn't help McCain. And the candidates, especially Hillary Clinton and Romney in the primary and Obama throughout, may have ". . . willingly relinquished any spiritual privacy . . ."

PART III: CONCLUSION

Over the past 40 years, religion reporting has gradually improved and been more integrated into straight news/current affairs reporting. Moreover, to an increasing extent, religion is understood by media professionals as interwoven in current events. Just think of the following topics: Islamic extremism, Jewish settlements in the West Bank, gay marriage, abortion, stem cell research, the teaching of evolution, presidential politics, the Dalai Lama's struggles with China, or the pope's speeches and travels. Consequently, a political reporter cannot cover his or her beat without an awareness of its potential "religion angle." Although such a reporter cannot be expected to be an expert on religion, he or she can be expected to ask the question: Does religion play a part in a particular story? If so, what questions need to be asked, what experts consulted, what resources (books, websites) checked?

Religion is a high-voltage topic, as I've tried to show, and will always present challenges to reporters. Yet, with reasonably careful research—especially in our era of instantly accessible facts online—consultations with experts on a paper's staff and religion scholars, and the conviction that the "religion angle," for good or ill, is here to stay, general assignment reporters should be able to successfully integrate this important dimension into political stories when relevant.

SUGGESTIONS FOR FURTHER READING

Berlinerblau, Jacques. 2008. *Thumpin' It (The Use and Abuse of the Bible in Today's Presidential Politics)*. Louisville: Westminster John Knox Press.

Eck, Diana. 2001. *A New Religious America (How a "Christian Country" Has Become the World's Most Religiously Diverse Nation)*. San Francisco: Harper.

Hubbard, Benjamin, John Hatfield, and James Santucci. 2007. *An Educator's Classroom Guide to America's Religious Beliefs and Practices*. Westport, CT, Libraries Unlimited.

Marty, Martin E. 2005. *When Faiths Collide*. Oxford, UK: Blackwell.

Murray, Bruce. 2008. *Religious Liberty in America (The First Amendment in Historical and Contemporary Perspective)*. Amherst, MA: University of Massachusetts Press.

O'Brien, Joanne, and Martin Palmer. 2007. *The Atlas of Religion*. Berkeley: University of California Press.

Paulson, Michael, et al., the investigative staff of *The Boston Globe*, 2002. *Betrayal (The Crisis in the Catholic Church)*. Copyright by *The Boston Globe*, Boston: Little Brown & Co.

Prothero, Stephen. 2007. *Religious Literacy (What Every American Needs to Know—and Doesn't)*. San Francisco: Harper.

Smith, Houston. 2001. *Why Religion Matters (The Fate of the Human Spirit in an Age of Disbelief)*. San Francisco: Harper.

SUGGESTED DISCUSSION QUESTIONS

1. In what ways can journalists highlight the importance of religion reporting in national politics in the wake of the demise of so many dailies in recent times?
2. What role can the media play in fostering the democratic process through reporting on religion?
3. Should news media provide more or less coverage of religious news and why?
4. What is the future coverage of religion in the media according to the study carried out by the research team funded by the Garrett-Medill Center for Religion and the News Media at Northwestern University?
5. Should more journalists be deployed by media houses to cover religion than is currently the trend?
6. Should news organizations even bother to cover religion and why?
7. In the light of the research studies enumerated in this chapter, what should be the tone of media coverage of religion?
8. Briefly discuss the role religion coverage in the media played in the 2008 presidential election. In what way, according to Professor Hubbard, did the press fail to cover the religious angle of this election?

ENDNOTES

1. B. Hubbard (ed.) Sonoma, CA: Polebridge Press, 1990, pp. 3–19.
2. Cf. Andrew Walsh, "The Twilight of the Religion Writers" in *Religion in the News,* Fall 2008. Retrievable at http://caribou.cc.trincoll.edu/depts_csrpl/RINVOL11No2/twilight%20religion%20writers.htm. Walsh also discusses online religion writing which Debra Mason's chapter in this volume analyzes.
3. See *Reporting Religion,* pp. 5–7.
4. http://mediamatters.org.
5. www.PBS.org/religion.
6. http://pewforum.org/docs/?DOCID=372. The Pew study extended from June 1 to October 15, 2008. It examined 7,592 campaign stories in 48 media outlets: newspapers, television networks, cable TV, news and talk radio, and websites. Somewhat surprisingly to me, the coverage did not include any of the three major weekly news magazines: *Newsweek, Time,* or *U.S. News and World Report.*

7. For a discussion, see Chapter 7 of this book, "Church, State and Media: Presidential Politics at the 2008 Saddleback Civil Forum," Alan Schroeder.

8. For example, Martin Luther King, Jr., in a 1967 speech during the Vietnam War, called the United States "the greatest purveyor of violence in the world today."

9. www.miamiherald.com/opinion/other_views/v-print/story/586100.html.

10. www.time.com/time/printout/0,8816,1837536,00.html.

11. Miller of *Newsweek* and Jonathan Darman (October 8, 2007) wrote an informative story about Romney's life and Mormon faith that struck just the right balance.

12. www.boston.com/news/nation/articles/2008/06/03/mix_of_politics_religion_appears_...

PART 2

Religion in the 21st Century: Technology and the New Specialized Reporting

CHAPTER 5

Religion News in the Age of the Internet

The author is director of the Center on Religion & the Professions at the University of Missouri, where she is a professor of journalism studies. She also is head of the Religion Newswriters Association, a professional association for journalists who write about religion in the mainstream media. Portions of this chapter were adapted with permission from Reporting on Religion: A Primer on Journalism's Best Beat (Westerville, Ohio: Religion Newswriters, 2006).

The U.S. news media's financial crisis is well known and well reported. Articles about the collapse of business models to support print and broadcast news are easy to find; a recent Google search of the phrase "newspaper crisis" yielded more than 55,000 results.

While publishers are experimenting with new business models, no one specific model has surfaced as effective in restoring the connection between newspaper content and increased revenue. Even after significant investments in technology, less than 10 percent of newspaper advertising dollars are from online sources. Some 70 to 80 percent of revenues are still generated from print advertising. As a result, a Congressional Research Services report quotes one newspaper scholar as predicting that roughly half of the 1,400 U.S. daily newspapers will close by 2020.[1]

The good news is that the online reading of news is growing and, according to the Pew Project for Excellence in Journalism's 2009 *The State of the News Media* report, online news site visitors outnumbered newsstand sales by more than 11 million people. Clearly, plenty of people still consume the news.[2]

Audience Interest in Religion News Remains

Although news industry trends have devastated the coverage of religion as a beat, religion news in the general media always has been limited. Content studies show it's typically less than 2 percent of the total space devoted to news. Regardless, as Prof. Ben Hubbard discusses in Chapter 4, during the economic boom of the 1990s, religion news enjoyed significant presence and growth. Newspaper faith and values sections became large and diverse, with complex and engaging stories.

Printed religion sections, however, were expensive and as papers began downsizing around 2004, most sections were closed or replaced with a token page. Similarly, broadcast religion news remained stagnant and rare. Yet despite trends for coverage of religion within the news industry, research shows significant audience interest in religion news and in religion online—a reflection, perhaps, of the well-documented religious adherence and practice in the United States. Surveys show six in ten Americans say religion is "very important" in their lives.[3] Religion is the No. 1 category of giving each year to nonprofit groups, according to GivingUSA.[4] Religious practices and rituals are a daily part of millions of Americans' lives and they seek religious information online.

According to a 2007 Pew Research Center for the People & the Press report, 35 percent of Internet users have searched for information about religion online; half of those have looked for information about faiths other than their own.[5] At *USA Today*, religion reporter Cathy Lynn Grossman's blog outstripped the paper's most popular blog in number of comments generated within two months of its start.[6] At the *Washington Post*, the "On Faith" blog—a collaboration with *Newsweek*—racks up hundreds of thousands of views each month, making it one of the paper's most popular blogs.[7] At *The Grand Rapids* (Mich.) *Press*, Charles Honey's columns have been among the Michigan-centric Booth Newspaper chain's most popular online offerings.[8]

New Skill Sets and Opportunities

As people are disengaging from traditional journalism—print and broadcast—they are engaging with each other through the Internet, whether it's Myspace, Facebook, or other social networking sites and blogs. As the sociologist Robert D. Putnam argues in *Bowling Alone*, the less engaged in civic life people become, the more they hunger for interaction.[9] With these shifts, the roles of journalists are shifting—and this is true of all journalists, not just religion reporters.

Or as Steve Yelvington, a citizen journalism guru, describes it, the gatekeeper now becomes a guide; the reporter becomes a participant; the town crier becomes a convener.[10] The skill sets all journalists need to know now, Yelvington says, are those of community-building, conversational writing, guerilla marketing, viral promoting, presenting skills, and group leadership. Technologies will change; but the need for skills does not.

So what does this have to do with religion news? It means that the core of how we define news, the nature of news, is changing. In the case of religion reporting, that's a good thing, because we've been caught for decades in conflict frames. We report the culture wars as literal wars, where the nuance—the soul of faith and values in the lives of real people—largely has been lost. Perhaps that's why, in the largest newspaper study—comprising 37,000 consumers and detailed content studies of 100 newspapers—religion ranked nearly last on a list of 23 categories of news, in terms of reader satisfaction.[11]

The elimination of a specialized religion beat at many media outlets presents great opportunities for every journalist in two respects. First, many meaningful, excellent faith and values stories are waiting to be told for the smart journalist who knows where to look. Second, it means opportunities for new, online niche religion site startups.

A handful of entrepreneurs and commercial businesses already have honed in on religion as an online opportunity, most of which include some sort of news. Every site with religion news can be categorized one of four ways: as an aggregator, information-only sites (think Wikipedia), social networking sites (like Facebook) and actual news sites. Some of these sites are well established; others are new experiments. Most of these sites do more than one thing, with their central mission something other than reporting the news.

The largest religion-only site is Beliefnet, with a reported three million unique visitors a month. Although Beliefnet once carried more news, it now focuses on inspiration, support, social networking, and advice. Most of its news is in the form of blogs on niche topics such as politics or Jewish life.

Another popular online site is Religion News Service, which sends a free newsletter with limited news items and plans to expand its free religion content in the future. Two largely grant-funded broadcast projects have their content and supplemental reports online: *Religion and Ethics Newsweekly,* which is broadcast on PBS, and *Speaking of Faith:* An in-depth radio show and multimedia website.

Entrepreneurial religion sites are growing, too. David Crumm, a former *Detroit Free Press* religion reporter, runs the small niche religion site, Read the Spirit, which is intended to appeal to people of faith, clergy, and religious media. ReligionDispatches, with substantial support from the Ford Foundation, presents a progressive religious voice by writers who are largely academics in the field of religion. In contrast is World Magazine,[12] with original reporting and commentary aimed at Christian evangelicals. Similar sites for every major faith exist—some online-only startups like Islamicity, of interest to Muslims. Other religion news sites are online versions of print or wire services, such as the Jewish Telegraphic Agency or the Buddhist magazine *Tricycle.*

The New Basics

Journalists practiced in looking for the religion angle in stories on every beat and in all media will earn a reputation for writing stories with deep and nuanced portrayals of reality. The ability to recognize great stories with religion as a component and appropriate sources can take years of practice. Fortunately, major grant funding the past 12 years has built repositories of sources, story ideas, and resources every journalist should know. These resources, as well as some common sense guidance, can assure that any journalist writes about religion with balance, accuracy, and insight.

Of course, you need stellar core reporting and writing skills to tell stories about religion. But today's journalists must also learn to create relationships, facilitate public expression of faith, and encourage civility in the community conversations that exist via the hundreds and thousands of blogs or user-generated content sites. These skills are now part of the new "basics" required of all journalists.

Writing about religion also brings some peculiar ethical and journalistic challenges, which we'll discuss briefly below.

Understand Your Own Ethics and Values

Journalists must decide how transparent to be about their own faith traditions when writing about any aspect of religion. Although political reporters, for example, are rarely asked which political party they favor, journalists interviewing people of faith will, eventually, be asked their beliefs. The increased use of blogs and first-person writing also means many people must decide how open they are about their religious views.

Religion is an intimate, emotional, and revealing topic, which is one reason it makes for such great stories. It's also the reason that sources and media audiences will be interested in what you believe. After all, journalists report on facts, but religions are based on beliefs that can't be proven or disproven. People's religious beliefs affect the way they vote, raise their children, and spend their time and money. Why shouldn't they also affect their work as a journalist? People who report on religion can be sure of two things: Sources will ask about your own beliefs, and you will have to report about people whose beliefs you disagree with.

While ethics and conflicts of interest are important topics for all journalists, journalists will find there are special considerations when writing about religion. Veteran religion reporters have various ways of responding to questions about their own faith; there's no single right way to respond. Journalists must handle questions in ways that feel comfortable. Some journalists also find they answer the question differently over time or in different situations.

One option is to be upfront about your views on religion. Some reporters say that they feel they need to be honest and open with sources because they are asking sources to be honest and open with them. Others avoid specific responses but answer in general terms, such as, "I'm Jewish." Journalists should try to understand the motivation for the question and make sure the sources are assured you will be fair no matter what your views on religion. Other reporters try to deflect the question or challenge assumptions of bias held by sources.

Know Your Biases

Just as you need to figure out in advance of a religion story how you will respond when asked about your religious beliefs, it's also vital that you understand your own religious biases. Most journalists have plenty of practice reporting about people they disagree with. Religion, however, introduces a new intensity to that challenge. It's one thing to be a political reporter who votes Democrat and interviews Republicans. But it's more challenging when a reporter's sacred beliefs are ridiculed by a news source who is tomorrow's lead story.

Journalists should approach the story not as though you are trying to prove a faith true or untrue—rather, have a respectful attitude when it comes to the validity of someone else's faith. By all means, you should ask hard questions about improprieties or abuses. But separate the actions of individuals from the principles of a faith.

Grappling with the complexities of faith is aided by a standardized approach that can help minimize biased or unfair reporting. Here, the late Robert Maynard's use of "fault lines" is useful, particularly as we try to be anticipatory, and not just reactionary, in incorporating religion in the news. Maynard, the former publisher at *The Oakland Tribune* and namesake of the Maynard Institute, believed that the fault lines of race, class, gender, generation, and geography are the most important forces shaping U.S lives and tensions.

For many, religion is an enduring fault line as well, although Maynard did not specifically include it in his framing. Much of today's media coverage breaks the country into evangelical or mainline Protestant, Mormon or Muslim, atheist, or religious fanatic. These superficial categorizations fail to capture the complexity of American life, including spirituality, that journalists need to portray.

The Maynard Institute "fault lines" framework can be used as a quick checklist for journalists planning their coverage of a community's character. Maynard says these questions help assure that an individual's personal biases are not cluttering the real story:

What is the story really about?
Which fault lines are at work in complex issues?
Which fault lines are dominant?
How do other fault lines factor in?

Whose voices are telling the story?
Who has been left out?
What are your fault lines?
How do your fault lines affect your work?[13]

Adding the word "religion" and seriously engaging each of these questions can help journalists sort out both known and unintentional religious biases. If you are unable, with the use of context, counterclaims and facts, to achieve fairness in your reporting, then consider bowing out of a story. Similarly, reporters should, if possible, avoid reporting on their local place of worship. But prohibiting a journalist from belonging to a religious group violates the person's First Amendment right to practice religion freely. There are, however, some clear boundaries. Promoting your faith tradition above others or endorsing its beliefs in any way breeches ethical boundaries.

Journalists also should not report on issues from which you cannot separate your religious beliefs. For example, if your faith believes that homosexuality is a sin and you do not feel you can impartially write about the role of religious organizations in state initiatives banning gay marriage, you should recuse yourself from coverage.

Humility as Your Hallmark

An honest appraisal of your faith fault lines as you plan and execute your reporting is vital. But equally vital is the ability to remove any assumptions about religious belief and practice. Just because you grew up Roman Catholic and understand, for example, the Catholic Church's teaching on a "just war" doesn't mean you understand that term's meaning in other faiths. In the United States, scholars have identified at least 63 separate Baptist denominations alone. The estimated number of religious groups in the world varies widely, but one encyclopedia counts 19 major world religions divided into 270 large religious groups and tens of thousands of individual groups. Within Christianity, scholars have estimated as many as 34,000 separate Christian groups.[14] Given the impressive diversity, it is impossible to be an expert in every religion. Rather than faking a level of knowledge you likely don't have, wear your humility on your sleeve and never be ashamed to ask about something you don't understand.

Be a Perfect Stranger

Unlike some other areas you may cover, etiquette is vital when reporting faith communities. It's an awkward feeling as a woman, when you extend your hand for a handshake and it's not met in return, for reasons of modesty. You should know in advance of visiting a house of worship if you need to remove your shoes or sit according to gender. And by all means, don't invite to a business lunch someone who is fasting, say for Ramadan, Yom Kippur, or Lent.

The most comprehensive guide to religious etiquette is the book, *How to Be a Perfect Stranger.* The book offers brief insight into key rituals and rites-of-passage ceremonies for more than two dozen faith groups.[15]

Such common and decent courtesies go a long way toward showing others you respect their beliefs and do not seek to offend. Journalists who visit churches, mosques, synagogues, or temples for worship and other gatherings should be especially careful in being respectful of rituals and practices. Common consideration and a respectful attitude can help your reporting.

In most cases, reporters find their visits go more smoothly if they call in advance to let the religious leader know a reporter will be present. There are, however, plenty of exceptions. For example, if you are tipped that the preacher is endorsing a politician against federal rules, you obviously don't want to let him or her know you'll be listening. Similarly, a meeting after a worship service may include discussion of a controversial issue, such as tearing down a historical building or splitting a congregation.

If a worship service is open to the public, you can consider what is said in it on the record. Sermons, in particular, can be quoted because they are public proclamations. Reporters should be careful about quoting prayers, however; people have filed lawsuits over their private problems being made public. If you're attending a worship service as a reporter, you are not expected to participate. Some reporters find it easier to sing during songs or close their eyes during prayer in order to blend in. Regardless, always ask permission in advance if you seek to record or film any portion of the service. Most clergy will restrict where cameras, particularly, can be located.

In addition, many traditions have particular customs or rules regarding what women wear and how they act. Some rules are easy for reporters to comply with, but others hamper your ability to report. Many mosques require women to cover their heads, and most reporters don't mind bringing a headscarf or donning one made available to them. Similarly, some traditions—Muslims and some Pentecostals, for example—expect women to dress modestly, so reporters intentionally wear clothes that cover their arms and legs.

When religious customs limit reporting, most veteran journalists handle restrictions with ingenuity and perseverance rather than confrontation. If women are not expected to approach men and initiate conversation, you might enlist a woman to ask her husband to explain your need to interview men. If men and women are segregated during worship, as they are in some mosques and synagogues, you might quietly try to reposition yourself so you can see the men's section. Some groups prohibit men from shaking hands with women. Wait until a hand is extended to you before attempting to shake someone's hand.

Grow a Thick Hide

No other topic gets critiqued more than religion news. Multiple blogs are devoted to critiquing the media's coverage of faith and values. No topic gets more letters to the editor or more mail in newsrooms. Be thick skinned and understand it's a hazard of delving into one of the most personal and sensitive topics on the planet. But never stop listening; while few things stir passions as much as faith and no topic is as complex, sometimes the critiques are correct.

Tools for Better Religion Reporting

More tools and training for reporting on religion are available now than ever before in the history of U.S media, thanks to a glut of grant money distributed during the years 1999 to 2008. The resources, all of which are free and available online, include (listed alphabetically):

American Religion Data Archives: A collection of survey data on religious groups, religious professionals, congregational membership, and more. Special attention has been paid to making the data accessible for journalists. Available at: http://www.thearda.com.

The Religion Initiative of the Council on Foreign Affairs: The Council on Foreign Affairs has created a forum to broaden the understanding of religion's role in foreign policy. It includes periodical reports, experts guide, newsletters, and other resources. Available at: http://www.cfr.org/about/outreach/religioninitiative/index.html.

The Pew Forum on Religion & Public Life: The Pew Forum gathers in-depth analysis, survey data, and transcripts from its programs for the most comprehensive source of data about religion and politics. Much of their work is aimed at journalists. Available at: http://www.pewforum.org.

ReligionLink: ReligionLink gives story ideas and the most extensive, topical source lists anywhere on the Internet. Lists of sources include advocacy groups, religious institutions, scholars, and other experts. The archives date to 2002. ReligionLink is published weekly by Religion Newswriters Association. Available at: http://www.Religionlink.com.

ReligionSource: The American Academy of Religion created this online, searchable database of more than 5,000 scholars of religion. Only registered journalists may access the data, which includes contact information and publications for every scholar. Available at: http://www.religionsource.org.

Religion Stylebook: Journalists relying on The Associated Press stylebook will soon realize it has scant information on religion. That's why the Religion Newswriters Association created a free Religion Stylebook. The stylebook includes a detailed section on religious titles. Available at: http://www.religionwriters.com/tools-resources/religionstylebook.

The Next Generation

Finally, an anecdote. Rocco Palmo is in his 20s, yet media savvy Roman Catholics have made his blog, Whispers in the Loggia, notorious. Palmo is a serious Catholic who lives in Philadelphia, where his father works as a journalist. When Rocco decided the priesthood was not for him, he sought to find a way to marry his passion for the church with his admiration for the journalist's profession. So Whispers was born.

Rocco, via his blog, has done something few traditional U.S. journalists have done: He's been able to break stories and inside goings on of one of the most secretive and difficult institutions to cover: the Vatican. Rocco gets tips from inside the Vatican, from U.S. clergy, and lay men and women. He writes in a way that is casual and entertaining, yet he adheres to journalistic values, by requiring at least three separate sources to validate a rumor or tip.

Now, Rocco will be the first to tell you that blogging is not a way to get rich, and in fact, every so often, Rocco asks readers for donations. But here you have one individual, working on a shoestring, affecting and influencing the coverage of the Roman Catholic Church today.

In this world we live in, religion can and will be found in many places we're not used to seeing it. Instead of bemoaning or being fearful, let's embrace this as an opportunity to enlighten coverage of religion, and in the process, enlighten the world.

SUGGESTIONS FOR FURTHER READING

Huston, Smith. 1994. *The Illustrated World's Religions: A Guide to Our Wisdom Traditions.* Harper Collins: New York.

Matlins, Stuart M., and Magida, Arthur J., eds. 2006. *How to Be a Perfect Stranger: The Essential Religious Etiquette Handbook.* 4th ed. Skylight Paths Publishing: Woodstock, VT.

Prothero, Stephen. 2007. *Religious Literacy: What Every American Needs to Know – and Doesn't.* HarperCollins: New York.

SUGGESTED DISCUSSION QUESTIONS

1. Why is etiquette an important consideration when writing about religion?
2. How does the availability of online resources improve the coverage of religion?
3. What steps should you take to minimize bias when reporting about religion?
4. What would you tell a source who asks you about your religious preferences?
5. Why do some say religion is the most difficult of all topics for journalists to report?

ENDNOTES

1. "The U.S. Newspaper Industry in Transition," Susan M. Kirchhoff, Washington, DC: Congressional Research Service, July 8, 2009, Report No. R40700.
2. "The State of the News Media," Pew Project of Excellence in Journalism, http://www.stateofthemedia.org/2009/index.htm. Accessed October 4, 2009.
3. "A Look at Americans and Religion Today," The Gallup Poll, Newport, Frank, ed., http://gallup.com/poll/11089/look-americans-religion-today.aspx. Accessed June 25, 2009.
4. "Giving USA 2009: The Annual Report on Philanthropy for the Year 2008," GivingUSA Foundation, Glenview, IL: GivingUSA Foundation, 2009.
5. "Pew Internet & American Life Project Poll, February 2007," Pew Internet & American Life Project, Pew Research Center, Washington, DC: Pew Research Center, 2007.
6. Cathy Grossman, telephone interview with Kimberly Winston, January 14, 2009.
7. Charles Honey, telephone interview with Kimberly Winston, January 16, 2009.
8. David Waters, interview with Kimberly Winston, January 15, 2009.
9. *Bowling Alone: The Collapse and Revival of American Community,* Robert D. Putnam, New York: Simon & Schuster, 2000.
10. Net Change: How the Internet Is Altering the DNA of Journalism, Steve Yelvington, 2002. The (Texas Tech University) Mass Communicator 32, no. 1 (Summer 2007), p. 20.
11. "The Power to Grow Readership," The Readership Institute, Northwestern University. http://www.readership.org/impact/power_to_grow.pdf. Accessed June 14, 2009.
12. Listed online as Worldmag.com, Today's News/Christian Views at http://www.worldmag.com/index.cfm.
13. "How inclusive is your coverage?" Maynard Institute, http://www.media-diversity.org/index.php?option=com_content&view=article&id=604%3Ahow-inclusive-is-your-coverage&Itemid=57. Accessed March 19, 2008.
14. *World Christian Encyclopedia,* David Barrett, et al., London: Oxford University Press, 2001.
15. *How to Be a Perfect Stranger: The Essential Religious Etiquette Handbook,* Stuart M. Matlins and Arthur J. Magida, 4th edition, Woodstock, VT: Skylight Paths, 2006.

CHAPTER 6

Covering the Big Religion Story

William Lobdell

The author was a religion writer for the Los Angeles Times *when something happened to change his outlook. His front-row seat at some of the biggest scandals in the news had given him a unique reporter's perspective. It began to affect what he believed, and eventually, his own religious faith was shaken. The experience led to his book,* Losing My Religion: How I Lost My Faith Reporting on Religion in America-and Found Unexpected Peace *(Collins). In the process of telling his story, Lobdell includes some wonderful insights on the craft of religion reporting and writing, especially on big stories. The following chapter is excerpted, with permission of the publisher.*

It wasn't easy writing about the faith of a true believer. Journalists like to trade in facts. In many ways, sports teams and courthouses are among the easiest beats for reporters because the action happens in real time, right in front of them. There is a clear winner and loser, and statistics to detail what happened. At the game, you can even watch instant replay in case you missed the action the first time. In a courtroom, you can get a transcript and other legal documents to refer back to if you're hazy on a point. On the religion beat, you're dealing in facts mixed liberally with matters of faith. It's drilled into journalists that, "If your mother tells you she loves you, better check it out." But such journalistic standards can't be applied to much of faith reporting. It's impossible to check whether God is real, or whether someone's conversion is authentic. Large portions of religion stories are ultimately unknowable.

Excerpts from pp. 79–84, 177–180, 181–184, 184–186, 187–195 from *Losing My Religion* by William Lobdell. Copyright © 2009 by William Lobdell. Reprinted by permission of HarperCollins Publishers.

It wasn't my job to prove the Lord's existence or the worth of someone's faith—unless its worth could actually be proven. I operated on the premise that God and their faith were real to the people I interviewed. This allowed me to slip into their skin and feel what they felt. David Waters, a *Washington Post* editor and one of the country's best religion writers, developed a list of Ten Commandments for reporters on the faith beat, which I followed probably better than the Bible's Ten Commandments.

First Commandment: "God is real. For billions of people on this planet, God is more than a fact. God is a central factor in their lives, their values, decisions, actions and reactions." This was easy for me. It was the reason I got on the religion beat.

Second Commandment: "God is everywhere. Don't think of it as the religion beat. The world is our beat. Worship attendance is 24 to 40 percent [of the American population]. But belief in God is more than 90 percent." I tried to find stories in places other than church, as they made for richer tales: the struggle of a Jewish father to get his son's prep football game moved from a Friday night because it fell on Yom Kippur; the controversy over a Muslim football league whose team names included the "Intifada," "Mujahideen," and "Soldiers of Allah"; and the success of UCLA scholars in building a virtual-reality theater that acts as a time machine, dropping visitors off onto the dusty streets of Santiago de Compostela in northwestern Spain in 1211 to tour the cathedral there.

Third Commandment: "God really is in the details. John Ashcroft's father, a Pentecostal preacher, died the day after his son was sworn into the U.S. Senate. 'John,' his father said to him the night before, 'I want you to know that even Washington can be holy ground.'" David's point is that stories about God can be found everywhere, even in throw-away lines in articles or interviews. Also, he advises us to dig deep in our interviews. I almost always uncovered the most revealing insights at the end of my interviews, when everyone was relaxed and less guarded.

Fourth Commandment: "God is the object, not the subject. You don't have to write about God (or religion) to write about the difference God makes in the way we live." This is great news for religion writers, because it means that almost any piece of news can be turned into a religion story. In July 2001, I wrote a front-page story about how church leaders were taking advantage of the $600 tax rebate Americans were getting from the federal government by asking their congregations to simply sign over their checks.

Fifth Commandment: "God is good. Behind many if not most stories of hope, struggle, sacrifice, survival, forgiveness, redemption and triumph is someone's faith." I found that if I probe deep enough into any dramatic story, I find religion near its roots. I did a story about a guy who ran across the country at the pace of a marathon a day (26.2 miles). The reason? He had prayed for a way to raise money for needy children—and he heard God tell him to run an extreme distance.

Sixth Commandment: "Don't just write for the Church Page. God created the world in seven days, not one. No need to cram all the God-related copy in one weekly

'Faith&Values' section or page. Write for every section. Write for every day of the week." I had a running competition with a colleague whose beat included Disneyland over who could get their stories in the most sections of the paper. In one year, I was able to get onto the front page and in the Metro section, the Sunday magazine, the Calendar section and the business section. (She still beat me.)

Seventh Commandment: "Don't take weekends off. Friday night through Sunday night is Game Day for most religion folk. You can't understand someone's faith unless you experience the public expression of it." I found this to be invaluable in learning about different faiths, though I tended to find my actual stories outside of the religious services.

Eighth Commandment: "Don't spend too much time in your head. Faith isn't just expressed. It's experienced. It's belief and behavior. It's intellectual, emotional, and, above all, spiritual." I tried to report on mystical experiences with the same level of objectivity as a denominational squabble. When the marathon runner said he was ordered by God to run across America, I wrote it in a straightforward manner, without a snicker. For context, I did contact those around him to see if his behavior had changed since becoming a Christian, and checked criminal and civil court records to see if anything turned up. But as for people's alleged interactions with the Lord, I simply reported what their experiences had been. I tried to follow the example set by Supreme Court Chief Justice William O. Douglas, who in 1944 wrote the majority opinion in the *United States v. Ballard* case. Guy Ballard claimed, through mass mailings, to be a healer and prophet of God (he also claimed to be Jesus, St. Germain and George Washington). The government convicted him of fraud, which he had undoubtedly committed. But the Supreme Court overturned the conviction, with Douglas stating:

> Heresy trials are foreign to our constitution. Men may believe what they cannot prove. They may not be put to the proof of their religious doctrines or beliefs. Religious experiences which are as real as life to some may be incomprehensible to others.
>
> . . . The miracles of the New Testament, the Divinity of Christ, life after death, the power of prayer are deep in the religious convictions of many. If one could be sent to jail because a jury in a hostile environment found those teachings false, little indeed would be left of religious freedom.

Ninth Commandment: "Fear not. Even God has editors. They might not always get what you're trying to do or say, but keep at it." Religion frightens a lot of editors, many of whom aren't used to the subject and are uncomfortable with expressly religious terms. For one of my early stories, I covered the harvest Crusade in Anaheim, California. The three-day event is designed to convert nonbelievers to Christianity. I wrote a line in the story that went something like this: "About 20 percent of the crowd came out of the stands and onto the outfield to accept Jesus Christ as their personal savior." The editors on the copy desk flipped over that line. They said it implied that Jesus Christ was everyone's savior. No, I replied, it said that these people accepted Jesus Christ as *their* savior. It was just a fact. That's what happened. That was the whole point of the Harvest Crusade. They thought the line was still offensive and wanted to change it to something like "About 20 percent of the crowd came out of the stands and onto the outfield to *express their new belief in God*." I actually had to appeal to some supervising editors to keep the reference to Jesus Christ in the story.

Tenth Commandment: "Forget the flood. Interview God. No matter the story, ask people about their faith and how their faith guides their thoughts and actions." For me, this is a derivative of Waters's Fourth and Fifth Commandments. I suspect that my friend had a hard time coming up with a fresh Tenth Commandment, and David Waters's *Nine* Commandments didn't have the proper ring.

Waters's Ten Commandments served me well on the religion beat, and the Seventh Commandment — thou shall not take weekends off — allowed me on a personal level to sample a wide variety of Christian denominations and churches and find where I wanted to make my spiritual home.

Investigating the Pastor as Rock Star

The Prosperity Gospel as a whole was flourishing, and two of the world's most successful operators in the world of televangelism were headquartered in Southern California, within a short drive of my office at *The Times*'s Orange County bureau: the Trinity Broadcasting Network (TBN), the world's largest religious broadcaster, and Benny Hinn, the world's most financially successful "faith healer."

Trying to penetrate TBN, I started looking into its biggest star, Pastor Benny Hinn. Meeting Hinn was like being in the presence of a rock star. He pulled up to the Four Seasons hotel in Newport Beach in a new Mercedes SUV. Two beefy bodyguards jumped out of the car to flank him, scanning the entrance for any threats. In the marbled lobby, two associates and two public relations men joined the entourage, their dress shoes clicking on the polished stone floor. All this for an interview with me.

Hinn, the flamboyant, self-proclaimed "faith healer," is a familiar figure to casual channel surfers: he speaks with a thick Middle Eastern accent, wears Nehru jackets and sports a swirl of salt-and-pepper hair that has been described as a soufflé. He is perhaps most famous for the seeming ability to send believers fainting backward with a flick of his hand as they are "slain" by the Holy Spirit. His physical presence and showmanship, displayed an hour each day on his television program, *This Is Your Day!*, were mimicked by Steve Martin in the 1994 movie *Leap of Faith*.

Hinn claims to be a healing tool of the Lord. His viewers and "Miracle Crusade" attendees are told that if they have enough faith — measured by the size of their donation — God will heal them. It's clear his ministry has made him a wealthy man.

It's less certain whether anyone has been healed. And it's known that a number of people have died after mistakenly thinking they had been cured, stopping their medicines and avoiding the doctor.

I was excited to talk with Hinn, who normally didn't grant audiences with the media. For months he had refused to speak with me, even by phone. But apparently I had gathered enough unflattering information about him and his ministry that he decided cooperation might blunt my coming story. For spin assistance, he hired A. Larry Ross, a six-foot-eight giant with the thickness of a retired NFL lineman. Ross is one of the country's Christian PR consultants, with a client list that includes superstar pastors Billy Graham, Rick Warren and T.D. Jakes. Ross brought his top lieutenant with him from Dallas for the interview.

I had known Ross from other stories I had worked on and always found him to be highly professional and competent. He portrayed himself as a man with deep Christian convictions who represented only the best clients within the Body of Christ. Ross's two premiere clients, Billy Graham and Rick Warren, are inspiring preachers whose ministries do awe-inspiring work for the sick, poor and lonely. The worst a cynic could say about them is that they encourage belief in things that might not be true. Even a critic would have to concede that they inspire a lot of good works. But Hinn?

Investigating Hinn wasn't easy. He calls his tax-exempt ministry a "church," freeing him from filing public tax documents. He forbids anyone in his ministry to talk to the media. He lives behind gates in an oceanfront mansion in Dana Point worth in the vicinity of $20 million. Even the names of his board of directors are a closely guarded secret. Hinn's ministry is nearly impenetrable.

Aside from the occasional investigation by the secular media, few people care to expose Hinn and his ministry. While legions of vulnerable viewers are being told that generous donations to Hinn's ministry will lead to a miraculous healing, most Christian leaders are content to pass by on the other side of the street, their eyes averted — like the rabbi in the story of the Good Samaritan.

Ole Anthony is among the notable exceptions. For years, he has been the premiere Hinn watchdog, which explains why I went to Dallas to comb through the dusty archives of the Trinity Foundation.

For Ole's operatives, the most productive investigative work is frequently the dirtiest: making "trash runs" behind the televangelists' headquarters, their banks, accountants' and attorneys' offices, direct-mail houses and homes. (Trash is public property, though going through Dumpsters on private property is trespassing.) Under the cover of night, Ole's troops jump into trash bins wearing old clothes and latex gloves. They sort through spoiled food, leaky soda cans and soggy coffee grounds in search of pay dirt: a memo, minutes of a meeting, a bank statement, an airline ticket, a staff roster. Those scraps of information, collected over years, can piece together a bigger story.

In looking into Hinn's ministry, they had struck pay dirt in a south Florida Dumpster behind a travel agency used by the pastor. They found a travel itinerary for Hinn that included first-class tickets on the Concorde from New York to London ($8,850 each) and reservations for presidential suites at pricey European hotels ($2,200 a night). A news story, including footage of Hinn and his associates boarding the jet, ran on CNN. In addition, property records and videos supplied by Trinity investigators led to CNN and *Dallas Morning News* coverage of another Hinn controversy: fundraising for an alleged $30 million healing center in Dallas that was never built.

I came away from Dallas with a treasure trove of information on Hinn, including video of the faith healer making bizarre theological statements:

"Adam was a super-being when God created him. I don't know whether people know this, but he was the first superman that ever really lived . . . Adam not only flew, he flew to space. With one thought he would be on the moon."

"You're going to have people raised from the dead watching [the Trinity Broadcasting Network, on which his show appears]. I see rows of caskets lining up in front of this TV set . . . and I see actual loved ones picking up the hands of the dead and letting them touch the screen and people are getting raised."

From Trinity, I received copies of documents smuggled out by employees sickened by what they saw within the ministry: invoices and other papers unearthed in the ministry's Dumpsters and contact numbers of current and former employees, as well as people whose faith in the ministry had not been rewarded.

Shortly after my trip to Dallas, I saw similar scenes played out at a Benny Hinn Miracle Crusade in Anaheim. Hinn's public relations handlers kept me in a confined area on the arena floor and never left my side. Yet they couldn't shield me from the simple logic of Hinn's operations: raise false hope, and extract money.

A Benny Hinn Miracle Crusade is one of the greatest shows on Earth. The free event usually draws capacity crowds at sports arenas and stadiums in the United States and abroad. It's easy to see why millions of people—especially those with crippling or terminal illnesses—get swept away by the promises of the charismatic pastor.

Hinn's healing service is a sophisticated, choreographed production that lasts nearly four hours. It includes a long warm-up featuring robed choirs from local churches, hip videos on giant screens and audience members shaking violently and speaking in tongues, overcome by the Holy Spirit. Everything is captured on television equipment that Hinn brings to each crusade along with his own production crew, using seven cameras and a staff of as many as 100.

In Anaheim, Hinn made his entrance during a rendition of "How Great Thou Art," stepping triumphantly onstage in a dramatic spotlight, dressed in a dazzling white suit. He could have been an angel sent down from heaven.

He started by asking anyone to come forward who wanted to believe in Christ. Hundreds of people, many already in tears, walked down the arena's aisles to the stage, heard a prayer from Hinn and were handed literature that included a list of nearby churches.

Next, volunteer ushers handed buckets to worshipers, who passed them throughout the arena, filling them with cash and checks—signs of faith, Hinn told them, that they believe in God's healing power. Hinn's ministry collects enough money at crusades and on television to generate about $100 million annually, roughly the same as Billy Graham's organization. (Hinn reportedly earns more than $1 million a year, lives in an oceanfront mansion, drives the latest luxury cars and travels by private jet, the Concorde no longer being an option. As part of my investigation, a former associate of Hinn's slipped two notebooks full of copies of ministry expenses, including massive American Express bills and pages of unexplained cash withdrawals for the faith healer and his family.)

After more music, Hinn started ticking off the healings that were taking place throughout the arena at that very moment. Within a ten-minute span, the pastor proclaimed that people in the arena had just been cured of asthma, cancerous tumors, arthritis, leukemia, emphysema and 22 other ailments. And believers lined up on both sides of the stage to tell the pastor that they had been healed of heart conditions, knee problems, osteoporosis, breast cancer, deafness and more. Hinn applied his touch to their foreheads, scattering them like bowling pins across the stage.

The real drama happened after the pastor left the stage and the music stopped. Terminally ill people remained, just as sick as before. There were folks with Parkinson's disease whose limbs were still twisted and shaking. There were quadriplegics who couldn't move any muscle below their neck. These people—and there were hundreds, maybe thousands of them at each crusade—sat in their chairs, bewildered and crushed that God hadn't healed them; their caretakers tried to offer some comforting words.

Brian Darby has worked for more than two decades with severely handicapped people in Northern California and often has experienced the disappointment left in the wake of a Miracle Crusade. Over the years, he told me many of his clients have attended the events, where they were swept up in a wave of excitement, thinking they were about to walk for the first time or have their limbs straightened.

"You can't minimize the impact of *not* being healed on the person, the family, the extended family," Darby told me. "They have a sense of euphoria at the crusade and then crash down. [Hinn is not] around to pick up the pieces."

Many people believe, as Hinn preaches, that God fails to heal them because their faith isn't strong enough. Maybe they didn't give enough money to Hinn's ministry. Or maybe they just didn't *believe* enough.

Sitting with me for the interview at the Four Seasons, the pastor seemed like an entirely different man from the faith healer I'd seen onstage the night before. He dressed casually in black, with designer sunglasses, leather jacket and black shoes.

His trademark hair had been brushed forward, bangs hanging over his forehead like Caesar. Hinn fiddled with his cell phone, which sported a Mercedes logo. The fingers that allegedly heal people were delicate, with manicured and polished nails. A gold wedding band, so wide it covered the bottom of his left ring finger from knuckle to knuckle like a piece of copper pipe, bore the insignia of his church: a dove, symbolizing the Holy Spirit, sparkling with a cluster of diamonds.

"I know me, and those close to me know me," he said. "But sadly, the outside world thinks I'm some kind of crook. I think it's time for me to change that."

He was quiet, charming, humble and introspective. We talked for three hours. I asked him a series of questions delving into his ministry's finances, his lavish salary and perks and the inability to prove his "healings" lasted after the euphoria of the event was over.

He admitted that even one of his daughters, then 11, had a difficult time figuring him out: "One day she asked me a question that absolutely blew me away—from my own child! 'Daddy, who are you? That man up there [onstage], I don't know.' If my own child is asking that, surely the whole world is asking that."

He told me that he had a heart condition that God hadn't cured, and his parents had suffered serious medical problems.

"That is a very difficult thing for me because I told my daddy to believe," Hinn said. "But he died. Now I don't know why . . . My mom has diabetes, my daddy died with cancer. That's life."

The way Hinn portrayed it, being a faith healer was a terrible burden placed on him by God. If not for the divine calling, Hinn said he would walk away from the job in an instant. I couldn't look into Hinn's soul, but from where I sat, I saw a gifted actor who parlayed his theatrical skills and feel for the human condition into the material life of a movie star. I didn't think for a moment he believed a word of what he preached—or that he was bothered that people who didn't get their miracle cure had died. I imagined him behind the doors of his cliff-top Dana Point mansion, giggling to himself at his good fortune as he looked out the floor-to-ceiling windows at the 180-degree view of the Pacific with surfers bobbing in the waves, dolphins swimming just outside the surf line and sailboats dotting the horizon. He had hit the lottery, his actions protected from the law by the First Amendment.

When my piece on Benny Hinn was published, I thought his donations would dip at least a little. I even hoped it would prompt him to clean up his act. I was wrong on both counts. His supporters had been indoctrinated in the belief that the mainstream media was a tool of the devil designed to bring down great ministries and men of God. If I had caught Benny in bed with a dead woman or live boy, it wouldn't have made a difference. CNN, HBO and NBC's *Dateline* have done devastating reports on Benny Hinn and his ministry, and Pastor Benny's career has kept sailing along. My article didn't stand a chance. Today, he continues to be, by far, the most financially successful "faith healer" in the world.

Besides a handful of secular media outlets and a few fringe Christian organizations, no one is bothered enough by Hinn's antics and the harm he does to people and the Body of Christ to call him out. Many fear the tight relationship between Hinn and the leaders of the Trinity Broadcasting Network—coming out against the faith healer would mean incurring the wrath of the world's largest religious broadcaster. The Christian media, whose voice could make a difference with believers, have shied away from most criticism as well. In general, the Christian media is extremely hesitant to undertake investigative reporting on Christian organizations, no matter how corrupt. Controversy—and the resulting loss of advertisers and readers—scares them. Several freelancers have come to me with their unpublished stories after Christian magazines rejected the material as too controversial. I started to wonder why my faith had so few people of principle.

'The Fort Knox of Christian Organizations'

My story about Benny Hinn was part of a larger investigation into the Trinity Broadcasting Network. From time to time I had received e-mails making allegations about the leadership of TBN. Often the anonymous message came with details about sexual impropriety, lavish spending and questionable use of donor money. But no proof was offered, and the senders rarely responded to my questions. Then I wrote a small, straightforward news story that involved TBN. Twenty-four hours later, a flurry of e-mails arrived in my inbox accusing TBN and its founders, televangelists Paul and Jan Crouch, of various misdeeds. I decided that where there was smoke, there might be fire.

TBN was the Fort Knox of Christian organizations. No reporter had completely penetrated it; the network operated with a level of secrecy the CIA would envy. The ministry is valued at more than $2 billion, generates about $200 million annually and beams its programming from dozens of satellites into every country on Earth. If a pastor can get a show on TBN (the waiting list is long), money pours in. What went on behind the scenes was a closely guarded secret. The network's founders didn't give media interviews, and their employees were told not to talk to the press.

Channel surfers probably know TBN by the image of Jan Crouch, who wears heavy makeup, long false lashes and champagne-colored wigs piled high on her head. She speaks in a singsong voice and lets her tears flow freely, whether reading a viewer's letter or recalling how God resurrected her pet chicken when she was a child.

Her husband, Paul, with his silver hair, mustache and bifocals, comes across as a grandfatherly sort. What he calls his "German temper" can rise quickly, however. He often punctuates a point by shaking a finger at the camera.

"Get out of God's way," he said once, referring to TBN's detractors. "Quit blocking God's bridges or God is going to shoot you, if I don't."

The Crouches' eldest son, Paul Crouch, Jr., a thick man with bushy graying hair and a 1970s-style mustache, has taken the reins of the television empire from his aging parents and is trying to modernize it. Already under the leadership of PJ, as he is known, the studio sets have gone from gold and gaudy to chic. The programming is tilting rapidly away from big-haired Southern preachers to Christianized versions of secular fare, including an *American Idol*-style reality show featuring gospel singers.

Together, the three Crouches make up TBN's entire board of directors, giving the ministry little outside oversight. Like a miner looking at rock formations, a journalist can survey the ground before him and see the potential for a good story: secrecy, concentrated power and lack of oversight. But digging beneath the surface isn't easy. Over the next two years, while juggling other stories, I traveled back and forth across the country several times to meet with sources, stake out houses, knock on doors late at night, comb courthouses for documents and even sift through piles of trash others had collected in order to produce a portrait of the TBN empire and Paul and Jan Crouch.

I received threatening phone calls. A man with a menacing voice asked if I would be driving my usual way home that night and warned me to watch my back. Another caller said that a private investigator had discovered an illicit affair I was having with a male newsroom colleague (not true). A pastor in Riverside, California launched a website devoted to "bringing me down" because I was doing Satan's work. He posted a series of lies about me (such as that my editors had kicked me off the story) along with personal information about my family and me. He solicited donations so he could hire a private investigator to dig up dirt.

I didn't think I was in physical danger. My sources, however, felt their lives were at risk. I talked with hundreds of people for the story, and more than a few believed that their phones had been bugged and that they were being followed. This was undoubtedly just paranoia, but some of it was bred by the culture at TBN—and us-against-them mindset. Either you were with TBN and Jan and Paul Crouch, or you were working for Satan. (The bunker mentality filtered right down to the viewers. I called fans of TBN, looking for their positive take on the ministry and what it meant to their lives. Inevitably the first questions they would ask was, "Did Jan and Paul say it was okay if I talked with you?" I was able to talk to many of them only after Paul Crouch, Jr. announced on the air that it was okay.)

I spoke with many former TBN employees and current and former associates who said that as Christians, they wanted to blow the whistle on what they believed was abuse of donor money and immoral behavior, but they just couldn't. It would be too risky, they said, even if I withheld their names. Several were so scared that they reported our conversation to TBN officials. I grew increasingly frustrated by this nearly uniform lack of courage be people who claimed to be devout Christians. I'd often find myself quoting Scripture to them to see how they justified silence when they claimed to know about abuses within God's ministry.

"What do you think Jesus meant when he told his disciples, 'If anyone wishes to come after Me, he must deny himself, and take up his cross and follow Me'?" I would ask. "Didn't Jesus warn repeatedly that the Christian life would involve sacrifice?"

But TBN provided a gravy train for producers, pastors, singers and filmmakers. Rank-and-file employees needed a paycheck. Almost no one wanted to risk what he had, even when I'd ask about Jesus' promise that "everyone who has left houses or brothers or sisters or father or mother or children or fields for my sake will receive a hundred times as much and will inherit eternal life."

There were some wonderful exceptions. A few workers had been concerned enough about how donations were being used to smuggle out documents showing lavish spending by the Crouches. And I did find several brave souls who felt it was their Christian duty to talk about what was happening inside TBN. First among them was a quiet, unassuming woman with a soft Southern accent named Kelly Whitmore. She had seen a lot as Jan Crouch's personal assistant for several years; she told me she fled the ministry in the middle of the night, fed up with the hypocrisy.

TBN officials painted Whitmore, then 46, as a disgruntled former employee, but that just didn't fit. She was sweet, polite, naïve, and had an unwavering sense of right and wrong. Her accounts were straightforward and filled with telling details. Other witnesses and documents corroborated much of her information. I talked with Kelly for hours, and she seemed to have only one primary motive: to shed a light onto what was happening at TBN. (She had retained an agent and talked about selling her story to Hollywood, but that seemed to be pushed more by her friends than by Kelly.) A lot of her information ended up in my story, but even more was left out, because in many cases I couldn't get anyone on the record to back her up out of fear of retribution. People didn't even want to be used as anonymous sources. Kelly and a few others stood alone, but they—along with hundreds of documents—were enough.

By September 2004, when my series of stories was published, I thought I had gathered information devastating enough to TBN and the Crouches that the ministry would be forced to reform itself. I had discovered, for instance, that TBN's patriarch, Pastor Paul Crouch, had secretly paid $425,000 to keep allegations of a homosexual tryst with one of his employees under wraps. TBN viewers often heard about the evils of homosexuality and how to battle the "scourge." In 1990, Pastor Benny Hinn prophesied on TBN: "The Lord tells me to tell you in the mid 90s, about '94 to '95, no later than that, God will destroy the homosexual community of America. [The audience applauded.] But he will not destroy it with what many minds have thought [He would use], He will destroy it with fire. And many will turn and be saved, and many will rebel and be destroyed."

Lonnie Ford, a former TBN employee, claimed that he was forced to have sex with Paul Crouch during a weekend stay at the ministry's cabin in Lake Arrowhead. Through his attorney, Crouch denied the allegations and said he paid a settlement to avoid a sensational trial and massive legal bills. TBN officials pointed out that Ford was a drug addict and felon. Still, Ford's story couldn't be easily dismissed.

Working as a mortgage salesman at the time of my story, Ford had been hired in 1992 to work in TBN's telephone bank in Orange County. Crouch took an interest in him. Within four years, Ford said, he was doing special assignments for the pastor. One such job was to drive Crouch to Hollywood and take publicity photos for TBN at a Christian nightclub. Ford said he and others in the ministry were surprised at the assignment because he wasn't a photographer.

"They had to show me—and I'm not kidding—how to work a camera," Ford told me. Crouch told him not to worry about it.

After visiting the nightclub, Ford said Crouch took him to dinner at the Regent Beverly Wilshire Hotel in Beverly Hills. Shortly after that, in October 1996, Ford said he and Crouch spent two nights at the same hotel in separate rooms. Ford said they worked out together at the hotel gym and ate expensive meals with bottles of wine and after-dinner drinks. "I knew what he was doing," Ford said. "He was seducing me." Ford was an openly gay man.

After checking out of the hotel, Ford said, Crouch took him to a TBN-owned cabin near Lake Arrowhead. It was there, Ford said, that Crouch first had sex with him. "I did it because I didn't know if this man was going to throw me straight out of that cabin," Ford said. "And I didn't want to lose my job. I was going to be in trouble if I said no."

The next morning, Ford said, Crouch read a Bible passage (Proverbs 6:16–19) to him in an attempt to reassure him about the night before.

> *There are six things the LORD hates,*
> *seven that are detestable to him:*
> *haughty eyes,*
> *a lying tongue,*
> *hands that shed innocent blood,*
> *a heart that devises wicked schemes,*
> *feet that are quick to rush into evil,*
> *a false witness that pours out lies*
> *and a man who stirs up dissension among brothers.*

Crouch told him that because homosexuality wasn't listed among the sins, the Lord wasn't worried about what they had done. Still, Ford said, Crouch warned him to keep the encounter quiet "because people wouldn't understand."

Ford said Crouch told him the ministry would pay his debts—about $17,000—and offered him a rent-free apartment at TBN's Tustin studios. He believed Crouch was trying to pay him off. Ministry officials confirmed that TBN paid at least some of Ford's debts around that time. They said it was an act of Christian charity that TBN performs regularly for employees.

Within weeks of the alleged Arrowhead encounter, Ford—on probation for drug-related offenses—tested positive for cocaine and marijuana. He was arrested in the fall of 1996 and sent to a drug treatment center in the state prison system. After he was released in early 1998, TBN officials refused to rehire him. Ford threatened to file a lawsuit alleging wrongful termination and sexual harassment and quietly settled for $425,000.

Though I had been on the religion beat for six years at this point, I still possessed some level of naivete. I thought when the news broke that Paul Crouch had paid nearly a half-million dollars to keep quiet allegations of a homosexual tryst, the TBN faithful would get in an uproar, demanding more information from Crouch and maybe even his resignation. Instead, there was mostly silence. Donations streamed in unabated. Then came my two-part series that detailed the Crouch's lavish spending, Paul Crouch's drinking (a Pentecostal no-no), their strained marriage, their ministry-owned mansions, ranch and dozens of homes across the country and the rest of their earthly treasures. This information didn't jar the fans of TBN, either.

In fact, my stories were used as fund-raising tools—evidence that TBN was doing God's work and that the devil (that is, yours truly) was trying to stop it. Of course, one way to fight this satanic attack was to give money to TBN, allowing the network to continue to spread the Gospel to the ends of the Earth, as Jesus commanded. In 2004, the year my stories were published, TBN raised $188 million in tax-free money, a slight increase over the prior year. Its profit: $69 million.

The stories weren't just ignored by TBN's fan base. Top-name pastors such as Billy and Franklin Graham, Robert H. Schuller, Joel Osteen and Greg Laurie continued to air their programs on TBN. Politicians, including Sen. John McCain, still used the network as one of their media platforms. And B-list celebrities, including Chuck Norris, Kirk Cameron, MC Hammer and Gavin MacLeod, never stopped using TBN as a way to stay in the spotlight.

In the Gospels, Jesus warns that what you didn't do for the "least" among us, you "did not do for me." (Matthew 25:45) That's pretty sobering news, whether you're passing by a homeless person on the street or watching idly as the poor and desperate are manipulated by pastors on TBN to send it what little money they have in hopes of a financial windfall. TBN pastors even recommend that those with massive credit card debt put their donation on a credit card—showing God an ultimate act of faith that will result in that credit card balance being paid off within a month.

I walked away from the TBN stories doubting God's call for me was to report on corruption within the church. It just didn't make a difference. Many believers couldn't be bothered with any bad news that could break the fantasy of their belief. They held a blind allegiance to their favorite Christian leader—whether it was a priest, a Mormon prophet or a faith healer. Those who could help clean up messes like Benny Hinn and TBN—such as the big-name ministers who appeared on the network or Christian journalists—turned a blind eye. This allowed a handful of pastors and the network to keep flourishing, and caused millions of viewers to keep waiting patiently for their financial blessing or miracle cure.

I didn't know what to call the arrangement, but it wasn't Christianity. Or if it was, I didn't want to be a part of it. I had lost my way.

SUGGESTED DISCUSSION QUESTIONS

1. What do you make of this statement by the author: "It wasn't my job to prove the Lord's existence or the worth of someone's faith—unless its worth could actually be proven. I operated on the premise that God and their faith were real to the people I interviewed."

2. Comment on David Waters's Sixth Commandment that encourages newspaper reporters concentrating on religion to try and write for every section. Also, how is that relevant today with a decrease in space devoted exclusively to religion stories?

3. What reporting practices and standards for verification did the author use in trying to establish the veracity of claims made against the individuals and organizations he covered?

4. Discuss the author's reporting on Benny Hinn, both in gathering background information and in attending a Hinn crusade, and how does he conduct the interview at the hotel?

5. Discuss the author's acknowledgment of his own naivete and his disillusionment with the reaction to his reporting on TBS.

CHAPTER 7

Church, State, and Media: Presidential Politics at the 2008 Saddleback Civil Forum

Alan Schroeder

The author teaches courses in television journalism as an associate professor at the Northeastern University School of Journalism. A native of Kansas, he began as a newspaper reporter, then moved into television as a producer. He has written four books: Presidential Debates: 40 years of High-Risk TV *(2000);* Presidential Debates: 50 Years of High-Risk TV *(2008);* Celebrity-in-Chief: How Show Business Took Over the White House *(2004); and* Writing and Producing TV News: From Newsroom to Screen *(2008). A frequent media commentator, he has been quoted as an expert by the* New York Times, Washington Post, Los Angeles Times, *and* USA Today, *and has appeared on ABC's* Nightline *and* Good Morning America, *the BBC, CBS, CNN, C-SPAN, MSNBC, the Fox News Channel, NPR's* Fresh Air, All Things Considered, *and* Morning Edition.

In May 2008, the Republican presidential nominee John McCain challenged his Democratic opponent, Barack Obama, to an unprecedented series of ten televised town hall debates—events that would take place every Thursday night of the summer at venues throughout the country. McCain's goal: joint appearances that avoided "the regimented trappings, rules, and spectacle of formal debates" and produced "the higher level of discourse that Americans clearly would prefer." In public Obama responded favorably, telling reporters, "I think that's a great idea."[1] Behind the scenes, however, the candidate and his advisors saw little to be gained from an extended series of high-profile bipartisan encounters, preferring instead to limit themselves to the traditional lineup of three presidential debates in September and October.

Under pressure to accept McCain's challenge, the Obama campaign responded with a counterproposal: a single town hall meeting on the Fourth of July; an in-depth debate in August devoted to international issues; and the three traditional debates after Labor Day. Rejecting this idea as insufficient, McCain continued to press for a roster of weekly town halls, until talks between the two campaigns broke down in an impasse.

But a joint appearance between the two major-party presidential candidates did take place in the summer of 2008, in a format and venue without precedent in American presidential campaigns: On August 16, Barack Obama and John McCain shared the stage at Saddleback Church in Lake Forest, CA, answering questions posed by Pastor Rick Warren, the head of a 22,000-member megachurch. The event did not take the form of a debate—each candidate appeared separately in back-to-back interviews—but for voters and the media, it provided a sneak preview of the fall debates. Of perhaps greater significance, the Saddleback Civil Forum on the Presidency affirmed the standing of religion as a campaign issue—and of Rick Warren as a powerful player in national politics.

As Jim Rutenberg observed in the *New York Times*, "It has taken a man of God, perhaps, to do what nobody else has been able to do since the general election season began: get Barack Obama and John McCain together on the same stage before their party conventions later this summer."[2] Why did the candidates accept Warren's invitation when they could agree to no other co-appearances? How did the Saddleback forum play out as a media event? And what is its legacy? The answers to these questions say a good deal about the intersection of religion, politics, and media in contemporary America.

Organizing the Saddleback Forum

All presidential campaign events pose daunting logistical challenges. As a live television show with both major-party nominees on the bill, the Saddleback Civil Forum doubled the complications.

In the early stages of the planning, Warren sought help from an experienced partner: the progressive interfaith religious group Faith in Public Life (FPL), which in April 2008 had hosted a "Compassion Forum" with the Democratic rivals Barack Obama and Hillary Clinton at Messiah College in Grantham, PA (John McCain, already the Republican nominee, was invited but did not attend). The Compassion Forum, in its serial interview structure and thematic emphasis on "faith and politics," closely paralleled the proposed meeting at Saddleback, but key differences existed as well. Unlike Saddleback, the Compassion Forum relied on a pair of journalists as moderators: Jon Meacham, editor of *Newsweek* and author of *American Gospel: God, the Founding Fathers, and the Making of a Nation*, and Campbell Brown of CNN, the network that telecast the program live. Audience members affiliated with Faith in Public Life also contributed to the questioning, introducing such topics as poverty, human rights, climate change, and HIV/AIDS.

In his original announcement of the Saddleback event, Warren named Faith in Public Life as a co-sponsor, and he told reporters that Muslim, Jewish, and Christian leaders from FPL would help him develop questions for McCain and Obama. This alliance quickly raised hackles among conservative Christians, who took issue with the social justice agenda of the FPL. Though the carping was mostly limited to right-wing websites, Warren began to distance himself from his partners, informing a Christian news organization, "(T)hey came up with the original idea, but . . . actually we're in total control of the format, the program, the questions. It's at our church; and so it's not their event, it's our event."[3]

In announcing the forum, Warren took pains to distinguish his role as interlocutor from that of campaign journalists. "The American people deserve to hear both candidates speak from the heart—without interruption—in a civil and thoughtful format absent the partisan "gotcha" questions that typically produce heat instead of light," Warren's news release said.[4] Implicit in the remark was a critique of the political press and its orientation toward making headlines instead of educating voters. The reverend had a valid point. During the primary season a number of news organizations had sponsored candidate debates, with formats and questions too often designed to elicit clash, not substance.

Warren's announcement sounded a second, more amorphous goal for the Saddleback forum: "While debates typically focus primarily on the candidates' positions and only secondarily on how they'd lead and make decisions, this Saddleback Civil Forum will reverse that ratio,"[5] the news release promised. What Warren failed to explain was how, in the course of an hour-long interview, he would be able to get two media-wise politicians to reveal themselves as leaders any more than they had already had.

In laying down these markers, Warren mixed good intentions with naiveté. A shift in format and tone may have been laudable, but in any high-profile joint appearance the self-interest of the candidates inevitably will trump the high-minded objectives of the sponsor. This proved to be the case at Saddleback Church, beginning with pre-event arrangements. In effect, the candidates dictated the format, insisting that the questions be asked exclusively by Warren and not by journalists or members of the live audience. The candidates also demanded that the discussion not duplicate topics dealt with at the previous Compassion Forum, and that a live feed of the program be made available to any media outlet that wanted to carry it. At this stage in the planning, Faith in Public Life quietly dropped out as co-sponsor, leaving the event firmly in the hands of Rick Warren. The title of the program also changed, from the Saddleback Civil Forum on Leadership and Compassion to the Saddleback Civil Forum on the Presidency.

The candidates' insistence on making Warren the sole questioner may have been flattering to the host, but it also indicated that the Obama and McCain campaigns felt unthreatened by his potential line of inquiry. Above all else, presidential campaigns are risk-averse. In any live, unscripted setting like a debate or forum, the candidates and their advisors strive to control the variables; at Saddleback both sides sought solace in the hands of a sympathetic questioner.

Clearly each man saw political benefit in participating in the forum, McCain as a means of shoring up his shaky relations with conservative evangelicals and Obama as a way to make inroads with Christian voters who tended not to vote Democratic. Furthermore, the two candidates had a personal history with Warren that left them comfortable in his presence. To enthusiastic applause, Obama had addressed the Saddleback congregation on World AIDS Day in 2006; both he and McCain had recorded messages for the church's global AIDS summit. Warren described the pair of rivals as "friends of mine," and pledged that he would endorse neither for president.[6]

As the first face-to-face meeting between Democratic and Republican presidential nominees, the Saddleback Civil Forum drew enormous interest from journalists. In the days leading up to the appearance, Warren embarked on a whirlwind media tour, obviously relishing his moment in the sun. In an interview on CNN two days prior to the joint appearance, Warren's self-absorption could barely be contained. "There are two groups that are really worried about me right now," he said. "One is the seculars, who think I'm going to establish a religious test for the presidency, which I'm totally opposed to. And then there are some believers who are worried that I'm going to wimp out on stem cell research, using fetuses, and abortion. Which means both of them don't know me."[7]

Saturday Night at Saddleback

At nine P.M. Eastern on Saturday, August 16, the Saddleback Civil Forum on the Presidency opened with a graphic: the two candidates juxtaposed against an even more prominent image of Rick Warren. Bounding onstage in a jacket but no tie, Warren began the program with a few explanatory notes. "We believe in the separation of church and state," he assured viewers, "but we do not believe in the separation of faith and politics." Laying out the ground rules for the evening, Warren said he would ask identical questions of each candidate, "so you can compare apples to apples." As per a backstage coin toss, Barack Obama would go first; for Obama's portion of the forum, Warren said, "We have safely placed Senator McCain in a cone of silence."[8] This last remark would come back to haunt Warren in the days ahead.

The conversation with Obama took the form of a moderately interesting interview that broke no new ground. The candidate drew applause for quoting the book of Matthew in answer to a question about America's biggest moral failing. He defined marriage as being between a man and a woman, which generated another round of applause from the largely evangelical on-site audience. But he punted when Warren asked at what point a baby could be considered to have human rights, calling the issue "above my pay grade." (Obama later expressed regret over this response, saying, "All I meant to communicate was that I don't presume to be able to answer these kinds of theological questions.")[9]

Toward the end of the interview, Warren posed a query that unintentionally revealed more about the moderator than the candidate: "What do you say to people who oppose me asking these questions?" Avoiding any direct mention of Pastor Rick, Obama politely replied, "These are the kinds of forums we need."

Punctuating the back-to-back interviews with Obama and McCain, the evening's "money shot" broke at exactly the halfway point: a 36-second photo op with both candidates onstage together for what the *New York Times* described as "the hug shown around the country."[10] The evening's proud host occupied a prominent position in the middle of the frame, visually inextricable from the men who would be president.

McCain's interview unfolded with somewhat livelier results. Unlike his opponent, the Republican nominee played directly to the crowd, pointedly including them in his responses and addressing them as "my friends." He displayed a superior perception of the theatrical nature of the event, speaking in campaign-trail sound bites instead of the nuanced paragraphs of his opponent. Unlike Obama, McCain correctly apprehended the forum as a TV show first and a political disquisition second.

Ideologically speaking, John McCain held a home-field advantage with the Saddleback audience, whose conservative politics aligned more closely with his own. Asked the question about when a baby's rights begin, McCain forthrightly declared, "At the moment of conception," drawing a hearty round of applause from the spectators. "I will be a pro-life president, and this presidency will have pro-life policies," the candidate continued, sparking further crowd approval. "Okay," quipped Warren. "We don't have to go longer on that one."

Displaying his TV savvy, McCain used the Saddleback platform as an Oprahesque confessional. He expressed regret over the failure of his first marriage and recounted painful moments from his experience as a prisoner of war in Vietnam. The candidate's biggest misfire of the night occurred over a question Warren posed to both men: How do you define "rich"? Obama had taken the opportunity to tease the reverend about royalty income from his best-selling book, *The Purpose Driven Life*, before settling on a figure of less than $150,000 per family. McCain, caught off-guard, cited a figure of five million dollars, reinforcing perceptions that his extravagant lifestyle had left him out of touch with average Americans.

Assessing the Forum

Five and a half million viewers watched the Saddleback Civil Forum on the Presidency—not an enormous number, but respectable for a Saturday night in

August. The big draw on television that evening was the swimmer Michael Phelps winning his eighth gold medal at the Beijing Summer Olympics, a climactic bit of history in the making that attracted an audience of 32 million.[11]

The impact of Saddleback, however, transcended the size of its initial viewership. Media coverage was extensive, as both straight news reporting and commentary. With no historical precedent to guide them, journalists tended to approach the story as a mini-presidential debate, declaring winners (McCain) and losers (Obama), selecting key moments to replay ad nauseum (the 36-second hug), and critiquing perceived mistakes (Obama's when-does-life-begin response; McCain's five-million-dollar definition of rich). For the most part the mainstream press downplayed the theological aspects of the event, leaving that portion of the tale to religious media specialists.

Some of the most incisive non-mainstream reporting came from Dan Gilgoff on the website BeliefNet. In his "God-o-Meter" blog, Gilgoff observed that the forum "hung largely on the hot-button concerns of the old Christian Right rather than the new agenda items of the supposedly post-Christian right evangelicalism. It was a poignant reminder that despite all the media hoopla about a burgeoning evangelical middle and left, culture war issues . . . still hold a special place in the hearts of evangelicals."[12]

Others in the religious media lamented that the forum had not been more enlightening on matters of faith. In the online edition of *The Voice* magazine, the historian John Fea wrote, "The evening at the Saddleback Church was revealing for what the candidates did not say. All those pundits and secularists who worry about another overtly Christian presidential administration can breathe a sigh of relief."[13]

For the traditional political press, the Saddleback story evolved in a decidedly non-spiritual direction when word broke the next morning that McCain had not, in fact, been ensconced in a "cone of silence" during the Obama interview, despite Warren's assurances to the audience. (Warren's first question to McCain at the forum: "Was the cone of silence comfortable that you were in just now?" McCain's response: "I was trying to hear through the wall.")

Less than 12 hours after the event, Andrea Mitchell reported on NBC's *Meet the Press* that "the Obama people" were asserting McCain had not actually been sequestered and that he "may have had some ability to overhear what the questions were to Obama. He seemed so well prepared."[14] Mitchell's comment provoked a stinging rebuke from the McCain campaign, whose manager accused NBC News of "abandoning non-partisan coverage of the presidential race."[15]

McCain aides confirmed that while Obama was being interviewed, the Republican candidate had been in his motorcade en route to Saddleback Church, and then in a holding room that lacked a broadcast feed. They insisted that he had heard neither Warren's questions nor Obama's answers. "The insinuation from the Obama campaign that John McCain, a former prisoner of war, cheated is outrageous," spokeswoman Nicolle Wallace told the *New York Times*.[16]

Warren himself waded into the controversy in an interview with BeliefNet's Gilgoff, asserting that McCain had not received an unfair advantage and dismissing the allegation as "sour grapes."[17] Larry Ross, Saddleback's spokesman, told the *Washington Post* that Warren had meant "cone of silence" metaphorically, and that the reverend's words had been delivered "with a chuckle." According to Ross, "There was no whirring glass bubble like Maxwell Smart . . . He was speaking to the integrity of the arrangement."[18]

In exploring the "cone of silence" issue, reporters also learned that both candidates had gotten an advance look at some of the questions asked at the forum. Larry Ross confirmed that Warren had passed along several of the questions to Obama and McCain word for word, and that he had also previewed a number of other general topic areas with the candidates. As the *New York Times* pointed out, Warren "did not share with his audience . . . that he had alerted the candidates to any of the questions in advance."[19]

Most likely these sneak-peeks stemmed from an excess of deference on Warren's part, and not any sinister motive. Viewers could observe clearly that the host went out of his way to put his high-profile visitors at ease. At the end of one of Obama's segments, just before the feed cut away to commercial, Warren could be heard telling his guest, "Home run."

Which illuminates the key problem with the Saddleback Civil Forum on the Presidency: In adopting an attitude of chumminess with the candidates, Rick Warren traded away the critical distance required of the occasion.

The Saddleback Legacy

The Saddleback Forum gave John McCain a boost at an important point in the presidential campaign, but it also raised the bar for him in the fall debates. Republican strategists had invested a great deal of time, energy, and money in depicting Obama as a media star with superior performing skills, thus positioning McCain as the underdog in their face-to-face encounters. In the course of a single night, Saddleback rendered this formulation inoperative.

Not that Barack Obama damaged himself by taking part. Though the Democratic candidate may have "lost" the debate in television terms, his thoughtful answers and placid presence lent him an unmistakable air of authority. And Obama gained points simply by agreeing to appear in a setting as institutionally unfavorable as an evangelical megachurch.

From a media standpoint, the Saddleback forum illustrates the bifurcation between political journalism and religion journalism. For the most part the mainstream national press covered the event as just another campaign stop, one that served as a prequel to the upcoming fall debates. The religious setting supplied a novel frame for the story, but the bulk of coverage emphasized politics over spirituality. In an analysis entitled "How the News Media Covered Religion in the General Election," the Pew Forum on Religion and Public Life posited this conclusion about Saddleback reporting: "Although the event provided an opening for the media to offer the public a narrow window into the moral compass of each candidate . . . much of the coverage devolved into a tangential debate over whether McCain or Obama performed the best."[20]

The religious media—in particular, the online religious media—presented more wide-ranging coverage, though much of the commentary took the form of screeds. One of the most trenchant critiques appeared on the *Washington Post*'s religion blog, "On Faith," where the guest commentator Susan Jacoby condemned the Saddleback Forum as an unconstitutional "religious test" for the presidency. "I tremble for my country when I reflect that both candidates were apparently eager to answer highly personal questions posed by a televangelist," Jacoby wrote. "The truly worrisome aspect of this event is that it may set a precedent for future campaigns, as the Nixon-Kennedy debates did."[21]

Was Saddleback precedent-setting, or an anomalous reflection of one religious leader's ability to work both sides of the political aisle? Undoubtedly the presence of Rick Warren at the helm gave the candidates the comfort zone they needed in order to risk the joint appearance. And it is fair to conclude that the event would never have occurred unless both campaigns saw benefit in taking part. Less certain is whether future candidates will feel similarly compelled to sit down with Warren or other religious leaders for similar discussions of faith and values. At a time when America's fastest-growing religious affiliation is no religion, the conversation with Warren may represent an exercise whose moment has passed.

Did the Saddleback forum constitute an inappropriate intrusion of religion into the presidential election? It is interesting to note that this question arose not in the mainstream media, but in blogs devoted to religious issues. The willingness of political journalists to accept the forum at face value suggests that matters of faith continue to receive sacred cow treatment in the press.

At a minimum the involvement of Saddleback Church in the race for the White House shows that staging such a high-profile event can be fraught with controversy, however benevolent the sponsor's intentions. The "cone of silence" kerfuffle and the revelation that the candidates knew some of the questions in advance made Warren and his operation look amateurish. And the host's inability to distance himself as moderator further undermined the effort.

Nonetheless, it is safe to say that Rick Warren, even more than John McCain, emerged as the winner of the Saddleback Forum. The event ratified Warren as the leader of a new generation of religious figures; this status was confirmed after the election when President Obama selected him to lead an inaugural prayer. In the last analysis, Saddleback's real achievement was not to raise the tone of American political discourse, but to legitimize Rick Warren as a political force to be reckoned with.

SUGGESTED DISCUSSION QUESTIONS

1. What was unusual about the nature of the forum at the Saddleback Church in the context of traditional presidential debates?

2. Why did the candidates agree to appear in this event when they had difficulty agreeing on joint appearances and debates previously?

3. In what ways did the Saddleback Church forum reveal the influence of Pastor Rick Warren in American national politics in 2008?

4. How did Warren see the forum and his role in it as different from that played by moderators or questioners from the field of journalism in other political debates or joint appearances?

5. In what way does the author believe that the aims of the sponsor conflicted with the self-interest of the candidates?

6. What does he mean by risk-averse strategies in presidential campaigns and how did the candidates advance them in this forum?

7. The author describes how the press covered the Saddleback forum. Do you think it should have been handled any differently given the unique qualities of the event? What about the ways in which the forum was handled by the mainstream press and the religious press?

8. "We have safely placed Senator McCain in a cone of silence." How did this remark by Warren come back to haunt him in the days after the forum?

9. The author asserts that Warren "traded away the critical distance required of the occasion." What does he mean, and what lessons might there be for you if asked to moderate a political forum as a journalist?

10. The author concludes that the Saddleback event "did not raise the tone of American political discourse." As a commentator assessing a political discussion at a church, what would you be looking for to indicate how successfully an event contributed to public understanding of a political campaign?

ENDNOTES

1. Letter, John McCain to Barack Obama, June 4, 2008; Jim Tankersley, "Traveling debates for McCain, Obama?", The Swamp blog, *Chicago Tribune* online, May 11, 2008.

2. Jim Rutenberg, "McCain and Obama Agree to Attend Megachurch Forum," *New York Times,* July 21, 2008.

3. Jim Brown, "Rick Warren on his upcoming presidential forum," OneNews Now website, July 23, 2008.

4. Saddleback Church news release, July 21, 2008.

5. Rick Warren, "Presumed Presidential Nominees McCain and Obama to Make First Joint Campaign Appearance on August 16 At Saddleback Church: Pastor Rick Warren to Host Saddleback Civil Forum on Leadership and Compassion and Question Candidates on Faith and the Common Good," http://www.rickwarrennews.com/080721_forum.htm.

6. Rutenberg, July 21, 2008; Ed Hornick, "McCain, Obama to face off with popular pastor," CNN.com, August 16, 2008.

7. CNN *Election Center,* August 14, 2008.

8. Transcript of the Saddleback Civil Forum available online at: http://transcripts.cnn.com/TRANSCRIPTS/0808/16/se.02.html.

9. Rick Allen, "Obama Regrets Abortion Answer," *Politico,* September 8, 2008.

10. Katharine Q. Seelye and John M. Broder, "The Obama-McCain Faith Forum," *New York Times* online, August 16, 2008.

11. Frank Rich, "Last Call for Change We Can Believe In," *New York Times,* August 24, 2008.

12. Dan Gilgoff, "McCain's Surprise Triumph at Saddleback," God-o-Meter blog, BeliefNet website, August 17, 2008.

13. John Fea, "Why We Learned Nothing about Faith and Politics at Saddleback Church," The Voice online, August 18, 2008.

14. NBC *Meet the Press,* August 17, 2008.

15. Mike Allen, "McCain protests NBC coverage," *Politico,* August 17, 2008.

16. Katharine Q. Seelye, "Despite Assurances, McCain Wasn't in a 'Cone of Silence,'" *New York Times,* August 18, 2008.

17. Dan Gilgoff, "Rick Warren to God-o-Meter: Obama, Dems Can't Just Talk Faith," God-o-Meter blog, BeliefNet website, August 18, 2008.

18. Perry Bacon Jr. and Michael D. Shear, "Candidates Got Advance Look at Questions," *Washington Post,* August 19, 2008.

19. Katharine Q. Seelye, "Who Knew What When?" The Caucus blog, *New York Times* online, August 18, 2008.

20. "How the News Media Covered Religion in the General Election," Pew Forum on Religion and Public Life, November 20, 2008. Available online at: http://pewforum.org/docs/?DocID=372.

21. Susan Jacoby, "Saddleback Church Forum: A Religious Test for the Presidency," On Faith blog, *Washington Post* online, August 18, 2009.

CHAPTER 8

Citizen Journalism and New Perspectives on Religion in the News

Megan McKee

The author graduated first in her class from Northeastern University's School of Journalism in 2008, and was a student in the period that followed the landmark 2003 Massachusetts Supreme Court decision in favor of gay marriage. As part of her undergraduate research, she spoke about faith-based perspectives with letter writers to Boston-area newspapers. Her interviews went beyond the news accounts, which were confined mostly to the legal and legislative maneuvering. Her reporting explored some of the nuances in ordinary people's thinking. New outlets for this kind of reported material now exist in blogs, websites, and other forms of citizen journalism.

Ted Bosen, a public defense attorney from Plymouth, Mass., is so well-known for his liberal views in the local courthouses that he often gets chased by people who want to argue over what they consider to be the latest abomination. The 57-year-old, a gregarious bear of a man, takes it in stride. He finds the attention amusing.

"They just love to corner me in the hallway and beat me up on one of the faux pas on one of my favorite liberal issues or politicians," he said. "I have been a punching bag or a sounding board — one or the other — over the years."

But his lighthearted nature belies his serious commitment to his job. He works long hours, for less money than he's qualified to earn, trying to win legal appeals for society's outcasts including drug dealers, drug users, and people found guilty of sex crimes.

Bosen believes in what he does, and thinks that the criminal justice system is fundamentally wrongheaded because the odds are stacked against the accused long before their cases are tried.

"I do feel that in general in this society, law enforcement is out of control," he said. "The only way you put a check and balance on law enforcement is by protecting defendants' constitutional rights. I used to believe like they did: how can you assist someone who may have done something awful?"

Bosen believes that drug laws are too restrictive, that there needs to be a single-payer universal health care system, and he has a pro-choice stance on abortion. However, to understand him and his beliefs, you also need to know one additional fact: he is against gay marriage. Not many people know this. In fact, Bosen says his courthouse debaters would be shocked if they found out.

I met Bosen while looking for people trying to make sense of the recent legalization of gay marriage based on their tangle of life experiences and personal beliefs. Massachusetts had just become the first state to legalize same-sex marriage.

The contrasts in the tone of some of the press coverage were evident in a reaction article about a battle on Beacon Hill in 2004. It was over a proposed marriage ban that eventually never made it out of the legislative session. This was just a month and a half before the first same-sex marriage licenses were issued. In one encounter outside the State House between a rollerblading gay activist who gave his name as Chauncy Chance and anti-gay-marriage activists, there was this reported exchange:

> "Get some treatment, honey," a woman told Chance.
> "I go to the Fenway Health Center!" he yelled back.[1]

In just a few sentences, we see a dichotomy of stereotypes: the flamboyant gay man versus the crazy religious person. It's compelling, it's funny, and the bottom line is that it keeps you reading. But, to grasp the thinking of average people—those who fall somewhere between the Village People and Fred Phelps's Westboro Baptist Church gang—I knew I'd have to dig further.

Luckily, newspapers also have a great democratic feature: letters to the editor. Among them are nuggets of realism and nuance written by people whose words have escaped the slicing and dicing of editors. These provide fertile ground for further reporting, the kind that most traditional mainstream news outlets have neither time and inclination to pursue, nor space and airtime to provide.

I combed through every single letter to the editor in every single Massachusetts publication with online archived content to find the people thinking seriously about gay marriage. Among the hundreds of letters I read, there was this from Bosen:

"I've been a Massachusetts Democrat all of my life. However, after reading the news that my party has endorsed gay marriage, I have quit. It's not about bigotry, but about maintaining social constructs and shared values in society as broad ideals for all of us to uphold and emulate."[2]

As soon as I read it, I knew I had to speak with him. I called him up to ask if he'd meet me, and he agreed. Before I met him, I did what's essential for any reporting assignment, whether a 300-word obituary or a much longer investigative piece. I worked to gain command of the background on the issue so I could ask the right questions and understand references to the many facets of the debate about gay marriage. I read every single article on the subject in the archives of Boston's two major dailies, the *Boston Globe* and the *Boston Herald*.

I read through the transcripts of the often-impassioned debates by legislators in the state's 2004 constitutional convention sessions. It is there that constitutional amendments, like the gay marriage ban that was proposed that year and later died, are debated. Matthew C. Patrick, a Democratic state representative from Cape Cod, was quoted as saying:

"My children and my grandchildren and yours will have accepted the concept of civil rights for all, and I will know that my participation today will be equally as important as the civil rights movement of the 60s."[3]

Another representative, Marie St. Fleur, a Boston Democrat who was the state's first Haitian-born legislator, told of being proud of being an American. She praised the legislative process and a nation, *that believes that protecting the rights of individuals is supreme.*"[4]

Like these legislators, it was easy to get swept up in the emotion of the moment and what it represented. So, when I met Bosen, I was stunned by the eloquence of his arguments. Prior to meeting him, I had perceived gay marriage opponents as backwards bigots.

But Bosen is a well-educated and thoughtful man whose beliefs are rooted in his Greek Orthodox faith, his legal training, his commitment to social justice, and his extensive knowledge of the mythological roots that have shaped our societal and cultural ideals.

Bosen is also a talker and when he's warmed up, he can pontificate about his beliefs for hours. The crux of his argument is that society's image of heterosexual marriage is shaped by thousands of years of shared values, and that the legal system cannot dictate a redefinition of those values from the top down. He doesn't see the legalization of gay marriage as a civil rights issue because he thinks that civil unions — Vermont's answer to the gay marriage debate from July 2000 until September 2009, when full same-sex marriages began in the state — afford the same rights as gay marriage.

Alongside these beliefs, however, he steadfastly refuses to condone the arguments expressed by some religious fundamentalists who claim the Old Testament says gay people are sinners.

"I'm seen as a bigot because I reject homosexual marriage but I reject even more that [gay] people are sinful," he said. He'd rather "live in a world with gay marriage than live in a world without gay marriage" if same-sex marriage was outlawed based on the Old Testament argument.

When writing this essay four years after my initial meeting with Bosen, I asked to meet with him again to see how he feels about gay marriage. His views are the same, except for one difference: he's rejoined the Democratic Party.

A look at the religious makeup of Massachusetts, considered one of the most liberal states in the nation, shows that Bosen isn't alone in his wrangling with the gay marriage debate. According to the Pew Research Center, Massachusetts, along with Rhode Island and Connecticut, has the highest percentage of Catholics — 43 percent[5] — of its total population. Gay marriage is officially opposed by Catholics, though the same Pew data show that only 18 percent[6] of Massachusetts residents believe the teachings of their religion have one interpretation.

Among Catholics nationwide, 45 percent favor gay marriage while 61 percent[7] favor civil unions, according to an October 2009 Pew Research Center report.

These figures show a few things. First, liberal people can co-exist with conservative thought; identities are malleable. And also, the greater support of civil unions over gay marriage among Catholics shows that people considering the issue of same-sex unions in a variety of ways — not just as simply "good" or "bad."

Of course, there are myriad religious identities in the United States. People learn from many faiths throughout their lifetimes, whether directly or through interactions with others. So I was excited when in addition to Bosen's letter, I came across this letter from March 11, 2004, signed by Reed and Virginia Stewart:

> "Since marriage is so personal and may be so imbued with religious meanings . . . it seems best to us to refrain from the meticulous definition and regulation . . . Let the commitment ceremonies be under the general licensing of the government . . .[8]

The Stewarts had come to think that marriage in the legal sense should be available to all people, and individual participants should decide which considerations of faith, ceremonial preference, or conscience to include. Gay adherents to Roman Catholicism, for example, should be allowed to marry legally in the eyes of the state, but comply with church doctrine or marry outside of the church. They wrote that they arrived at this conclusion by reflecting on their past work as missionaries, their religious study, and their friendships and associations with people of many faiths and beliefs.

I saw in the Stewarts' letter the same type of thoughtfulness that Bosen showed through his words, and interviewed the couple in their home south of Boston. Both Reed and Virginia Stewart have the long and varied backgrounds typical of people in their 60s. Both were married once before they found each other, and together brought eight grown children to their partnership.

In his younger years, Reed was an Episcopalian missionary in Liberia. He realized while still young that he "didn't have the gift of faith" and now identifies himself as "a reluctant agnostic." He earned a doctorate in cultural geography, a field of study not unlike anthropology, and specialized in the geography of cultures and religions of Africa. He was appointed a professor at Bridgewater State College in 1970.

Virginia grew up in South Boston, where her family and most of her neighbors were Catholics. She remained a "cafeteria Catholic"—one who picks among different doctrines and keeps only those that are appealing—but stopped attending church after her three children were grown. She joined the Episcopal Church a few years before we met, finding that denomination "similar to the Catholic Church . . . but liberal enough to make me happy."

At the outset of the hour and a half interview, Virginia said this: "I don't ever think I make decisions about moral issues one way or the other because of my religious background." But as the interview progressed, her words told a different truth.

I asked the Stewarts to speak about the concept of civil unions versus gay marriage, and whether they thought one or the other was more acceptable. Both said marriage was ideal because it gives gay couples equal endorsement; for them, civil unions establish a separate class of existence for gays. Yet they drew the distinction between marriage in the eyes of the state and church-sanctioned marriage. Virginia used an experience from her adolescence to demonstrate her belief that these two things don't need to be aligned as long as equal legal rights are shared by all.

When Virginia was in her late teens, one of her good friends came home and told his Irish Catholic family he was marrying a Jewish girl. His family was devastated. Virginia said, "There was just crying; there was gnashing of teeth, because, if you were, as his mother was, a deeply religious person, he would be living in sin."

Virginia chose this story to show how commonplace values derived from church teachings can change over just one generation. In this case it was that a Catholic shouldn't marry a non-Catholic. To me, Virginia's story feels straight from a bygone era, like looking at a black-and-white photograph. I can see the facts, but not feel the full breadth of emotion because though Jews still can't marry in the Roman Catholic Church, inter-religious marriages are the norm. Virginia's implied message was that the next generation will find teeth-gnashing over gay marriage just as quaint, even if same-sex couples are barred from the altar.

For many, reading concerns from opponents of same-sex marriage like Bosen provokes a similar reaction: acknowledgement but no understanding. While I haven't gone back and interviewed elders about inter-religious marriage scandals, I did have the opportunity through this project to explore what makes a few people think the ways they do.

While I don't agree with Bosen, he made me realize the fallacy in making assumptions about people based on only a few of their viewpoints. It's possible to have co-existing liberal, conservative, and moderate values.

In fact, over time, I've come to respect the opinions of people who defy easy categorization because I now equate holding a variety of opinions with critical thinking. Conversely, I bristle when I encounter those who only parrot the official lines of their ideological affiliations. Through Bosen, I also learned how much we lose when we limit our understanding of issues to opposing extremes.

In traditional newspaper coverage, space is limited. For an average story in the *Boston Globe,* a reporter may have 1,000 words to cover a topic, which means he or she must make tough choices about what material to include. Combine that with the pressure to make an article compelling and it's easy to see why thoughtful people like Bosen are left out of the news.

This not only detracts from our understanding of major issues, but it does a disservice to the complex humanity underlying those issues. By creating stereotypes of people through mass communications, we create expectations for how people with certain characteristics will behave, act, or think. For Bosen, it means he can't have meaningful conversations with his friends about gay marriage because as soon as he broaches the topic, his friends assume he's a small-minded bigot who believes gay people are sinners.

"People shut you off," said Bosen. "They brand you." Never mind that he worked for as a long-time as an aide for a high-powered gay Massachusetts politician (he didn't want to name the person because he or she never came out of the closet) or has a close relationship with his gay sister-in-law.

Since I first met Bosen in 2005, much has happened. Massachusetts was the first in a string of states to take up the issue of gay marriage. California legalized it in June 2008, but within five months, voters amended the state's constitution with a gay marriage ban. In November 2008, same-sex marriage started in Connecticut, followed by Iowa in April 2009, Vermont in September 2009, and New Hampshire in January 2010.

From April 6 to April 10, 2009, the week that Vermont legalized same-sex marriage and Washington, DC, voted to recognize same-sex marriages, 26 percent of links posted on blogs and social media websites were about same-sex marriage, according to a report by Pew's Project for Excellence in Journalism.[9]

During the same week, only 1 percent of traditional news media coverage was devoted to the topic.

A month and a half later, from May 25 to May 29, the blogosphere versus traditional media gap became even wider when the California Supreme Court upheld a ban on same-sex marriage. That week, 35 percent of blog and social media links led to news stories about same-sex marriage while traditional media devoted just 5 percent of its news hole to coverage of the subject.[10]

The gap between the interests and focus of traditional media and media users is clear.

Now we're in the midst of a digital media revolution that offers an unprecedented ability to publish exhaustive material online. Reporters producing online content and citizen bloggers no longer are bound by the space limitations that plague print reporters. Instead of relying on a reporter to interpret material, media consumers can hear directly from people via online writing, video, and audio.

All of this has come with the democratization of the Internet through two-way communication tools like Twitter and the comments sections on blog posts and online articles.

The kinds of viewpoints that I uncovered through my reporting have a better chance of surfacing on citizen journalism sites or in blogs than they did in the past through traditional media outlets. In fact, it's possible for the first time to take this material and develop entirely new arenas for practicing journalism. This can be through interactive discussion for local websites or reporters' own blogs.

Thanks to technology, we now have the resources to cover big, society-altering issues in a way that more accurately reflects truth: with nuance. With gay marriage, for instance, a site could be set up that culls data about beliefs and turns it into interactive mapping software.

Writers and multimedia practitioners could produce in-depth profiles of people — whether decisionmakers or average people — through words, video, slideshows, or a combination. A section could lead readers to Twitter users who follow the debate. There would be an interactive state-by-state history timeline and narrative to help people visualize developments. And there could be a discussion board for people to process all of the information and engage with others.

Gay marriage is just one topic among many topics that deserve comprehensive attention. Bosen and the Stewarts are just a few voices among endless who should be heard. I chose to write about them for this essay because they stood out when I read through hundreds of pages of transcripts, articles, and letters to the editor that contained the words of legislators, leaders, and citizens.

For space and other considerations in writing this chapter, I chose them because their voices had a refreshing tone of thoughtful reasoning. Obviously there were other interviewing possibilities that could have been used for blogs or other citizen journalism platforms. The next generation of reporters has the tools to tell these stories in a more authentic way than has ever been possible.

Since I graduated from journalism school, I've been a regular freelancer for the *Boston Globe*. In that time, I've grown in ways that were impossible to replicate by writing school papers. I've had the chance to write about a multitude of topics and personalities, to find sources and stretch outside of my comfort level, all on deadline and without any handholding.

One thing that has been a constant through my education, career, and personal interactions is that I never assume I understand anyone's beliefs. By adhering to this principle, I maintain curiosity about everyone I meet. I'm able to ask the most basic questions of people, and through this, learn not just *what* they believe but *why* they believe it. And this, I've learned, is what's truly fascinating.

SUGGESTED DISCUSSION QUESTIONS

1. The author concludes that certain limitations on mainstream media coverage can produce stories that lack nuance. Discuss how you can think this can happen and why. In what way can letters to the editor and interactivity in digital formats provide a fuller discussion?

2. Think of three issues, whether local or national, that tend to have polarizing coverage in the national media. How has the coverage affected your perception of the issues? How influential do you think mainstream coverage is in shaping people's opinions and the outcome of policy debates?

3. Are there any issues where you think polarizing coverage is justified? If so, why?

4. What are some ways that the reporting the author did in 2005 could have been enhanced through new technology and media platforms?

5. What would be the ideal way to cover a "hot button" issue like gay marriage or the death penalty in a particular state?

ENDNOTES

1. Kevin Joy, "A battle just begun for supporters, foes," *Boston Globe,* March 30, 2004.

2. Ted Bosen, letter to the editor, *Boston Globe,* May 29, 2005.

3. *Boston Globe,* "Lawmakers speak out, pro and con, on proposed amendment," March 30, 2004.

4. Ibid.

5. The Pew Forum on Religion & Public Life, "U.S. Religious Landscape Survey," http://religions.pewforum.org/maps (accessed October 2, 2009).

6. Ibid.

7. Pew Research Center for the People and the Press, "Majority Continues to Support Civil Unions," October 9, 2009, http://people-press.org/report/553/same-sex-marriage (accessed October 15, 2009).

8. Reed and Virginia Stewart, letter to the editor, *The Patriot Ledger,* March 9, 2004.

9. Pew Research Center's Project for Excellence in Journalism, "Same-Sex Marriage Dominates Conversation in the Blogosphere," http://www.journalism.org/index_report/samesex_marriage_dominates_conversation_blogosphere (accessed February 18, 2010).

10. Pew Research Center's Project for Excellence in Journalism, "Ruling on Prop 8 Triggers the Online Debate," http://www.journalism.org/index_report/ruling_prop_8_triggers_online_debate (accessed February 18, 2010).

PART 3

Covering America's Dynamic Religious Landscape

CHAPTER 9

Memo on the Religious and Moral Center

Stephen Burgard

The author is director of the School of Journalism at Northeastern University in Boston and editor of this book. He is a former member of the editorial board of the Los Angeles Times, *and worked in daily journalism for 26 years before becoming a professor. His 1997 book,* Hallowed Ground, *explored the nation's new religious diversity, and the capacity of religion to unify rather than divide the nation. He teaches courses in journalism ethics and standards.*

The announcement that James Dobson had relinquished leadership of Focus on the Family in early 2009 prompted a short but incisive blog analysis from the *Washington Post's* "On Faith" editor David Waters.[1] Dobson has been a leading religious conservative with a high media profile and considerable political clout for his conservative stands on abortion and homosexuality. Admired and disliked on opposite ends of the political spectrum, he had become a poster person for the religious right, one of a handful of prominent names associated with religious conservatives during the "culture war" that raged across talk radio and media outlets from the 1980s into the early part of the 21st century.[2]

Waters began with the customary changing-of-guard explanations that one might expect to find in a report on the outgoing leader of a movement who had reached age 72. But in the estimation of the writer, there was more going on than a generational torch-passing. Waters pointed out that Dobson's retirement had revealed some dynamics of religious voters.

That world was more diverse than often portrayed. Dobson could sway the older leadership of the Republican Party, but his influence with younger and more tech-savvy and suburban-based evangelicals was less certain by the end of 2008. His tepid support for Sen. John McCain was seen as a reason for the candidate to choose Alaska Gov. Sarah Palin as his running mate. That political calculation didn't really pan out; when the time came to vote, evangelical support for the Republican presidential ticket was less than Republican leaders had hoped. Perhaps most significant, younger evangelicals were showing interest in more than the narrow social agenda of Dobson, drawn also to broader issues, such as the environment, global poverty, and AIDS.

This short blog managed to identify a fluid religious center somewhere between religious right and religious or agnostic left. These people do not always act in predictable ways politically; they are spread across the major parties, or they may be unaffiliated voters who are religious. They may take some but not all of their cues from leading religious conservatives if they are Republicans, or from church leaders if they are Democrats. In the end, they tend to think things through for themselves.

This group essentially has been a mystery to many journalists. The political center gets media attention, but not often for its tie to faith or religious and spiritual concerns that might shape attitudes and influence decisions. News accounts on the religious voter have tended to focus on the clout of TV evangelists and other high-profile religious conservatives such as Dobson, and on their presumed ability to rally voters around hot-button issues, to deliver them reliably in blocks.

This perception held true during much of the early going in the 2008 presidential campaign. The coverage on religious conservatives focused on the testy relationships between McCain and top evangelical leaders, and what that might mean for the election results. This was consistent with reporting on religious voters that often has them marching in lockstep with leaders known to the general public through talk radio and TV.

There is an important back story here. It turns out that while the press first was writing about the "culture war", there were two largely unreported trends that had important religious and political ramifications. The first was a kind of new religion-driven American pragmatism. It developed in the neighborhoods of cities and suburbs, and was made up of people willing to table theological differences to address common problems of gangs and deteriorating social fabric through interfaith initiatives. The second was a profound shift in the makeup of the American religious population that gave it a more global cast both in terms of both its composition and the world views of the faithful.[3]

The new religious face of America actually had started taking shape decades earlier with tides of immigration. With this came some changing attitudes about religion and American life. At the same time these shifts were taking place, busy newsrooms hewed more predictably to manageable stories, the religious right versus the secular left, and the warring factions within the Republican Party. Few reporters, editors, and producers had the time or resources either to mine survey research or do their own field reporting to see how religious belief was informing views on social issues and politics across a broader spectrum of the American electorate.

Just who is this group, the religious and moral center? It is made up of people who may not think of themselves as part of a movement or a party. If they are in the major parties, they tend to be conservative Democrats or suburban Republicans. They may be registered as unaffiliated voters. They can move in and out of the middle ground, allying as individuals with different causes and candidates, and even changing their minds on occasions. If you asked them for self-definition, it seems unlikely that the adjective "religious" would appear in front of the noun "centrist" as in, "I would say I'm a religious centrist." Faith gets factored in, but it is not always worn on the sleeve in thinking and talking about civic and political matters.[4]

The abundance of survey research today is a help in understanding this group and provides some confirmation of its existence. Journalists now have available an extensive body of polling that has dots waiting to be connected. This can identify segments of the population not confined to far-right conservatives, but for whom religion also is important. This group doesn't neatly fit the anti-abortion, pro-gun, anti-gay marriage stereotype of the religious right.

In 2007, for example, a major review of the religious population was undertaken by the Pew Forum on Religion and Public Life's U.S. Religious Landscape Survey.[5] This survey uncovered a discernible pragmatic streak in the outlook of believers. For example, many Americans were found to have different perspectives even within particular faiths. They were inclined to recognize that others may hold truths or the keys to salvation. They believed there may be different ways of interpreting church teaching.

Some recent polling by the Pew Forum suggests that increasing numbers of religious Americans attend services at places of worship other than their own; are comfortable adopting portions of concepts such as reincarnation that they find in other traditions; and engage in mixed marriages.[6]

Even with these changes, there is an underlying comfort level with religion for many. The American Religious Identification Survey, 2001, done by The Graduate Center, City University of New York, found 75 percent of the population either religious or somewhat religious, with only 16 percent secular or somewhat secular. For all the agonizing over the separation of church and state, they have strong religious beliefs; it is a predominantly Christian country by the numbers, and there is a curiosity if not always a knowledge about religious groups. A CBS poll from May 20–23 2004 found some 90 percent were okay with "in God We Trust" on coins, and about 78 percent comfortable with non-denominational prayer at public events. Seventy-two percent wanted the president to have strong religious beliefs.

The Pew Forum has been a leader in explaining what it sets out to map, the U.S. religious landscape. All of these people have kitchen-table conversations about the economy, the environment, health care, abortion, gay marriage, and other issues, and they vote. If such findings are used as background research for journalists looking into voting choices and attitudes on controversial social issues, some insight can be gained. By being aware of the larger terrain and making connections, the sort of conclusion about Dobson made by *the Post's* blogger suddenly is less of a surprise. This kind of understanding can lead to reporting that accounts more for the complexity and richness of the nation's large religious population.

The inability to factor in the faith-based perspective in the ordinary electorate has hampered the effectiveness of the press in earlier election cycles. This was so in the 2004 presidential election, with the emergence of what was called the "Values Voter." Days after George W. Bush's re-election victory, *The Washington Post's* press critic Howard Kirtz wrote about how a press stung by premature projections back in the 2000 election missed the importance of values and religion to ordinary voters four years later.[7]

The religious voter continues to be a bit of a wild card. The election of Scott Brown in January of 2010 to replace the late Sen. Edward M. Kennedy in Massachusetts brought its own round of national analysis of voting decisions made by independent and conservative voters. Much of the focus rightly belonged on the economy and national priorities. However, given the many Catholics in the state's voting population, there were religious elements in the nuanced position Brown (a member of the Christian Reformed Church in North America) had on abortion.[8] This had significance because of position shifts on abortion coverage and health care plans during the entire campaign by his defeated opponent, Martha Coakley.[9] It seems likely that faith-based considerations may have been at play for the electorate in a contentious corner of a special election that had national significance. In early March of 2010, concern in the health care debate over language restricting insurers' ability to cover abortion services became a point of disagreement between liberals and moderates in the House, as members of Congress looked ahead to the fall elections.[10]

In the 2004 presidential campaign, there had been limited attention to the significance of religious concerns; for example, there was some reporting on the GOP strategy of targeting Christian evangelicals and Catholics in battleground states. But for journalists, the importance of "values" to voters was most evident at the end, in exit polling that asked voters what really mattered in choosing a president. Of those who gave values as the top concern, the overwhelming number voted for Bush.

The press discovered this in its own survey, a poll conducted for the National Election Pool, a consortium of ABC News, The Associated Press, CBS News, CNN, Fox News, and NBC News. For anyone thinking, quite accurately, that "moral values" also can be a vague, all-encompassing term, there was a convincing suggestion that these voters generally had religious values in mind. *The New York Times'* account of the poll results made it clear that Bush had run very well in almost all categories of religious voters.[11]

Kurtz checked with some leading media observers after the election to find out what happened, and was given some of these explanations:

> "Bush did a very good job of creating some wedge issues on the moral values front," said then-CBS correspondent John Roberts. "That was a real surprise, something we didn't catch on to until late in the game. We all kind of missed the boat on that."

> "Journalists don't understand red-state America," said *Newsweek's* Howard Fineman. "I'm an indicted co-conspirator . . . Most people in what is left of the big media live and work in blue-state America, and that shaped our view of the election."[12]

The press at times had done an adequate job in covering the "culture war," but often seemed at loose ends in reporting on the large group of Americans who occupy the faith-based center. Such exit polling in the election of 2004 found these correspondents and many news organizations scrambling to account for the preoccupation with "moral values" that turned up, not on the far right of American politics, but among mainstream voters.

This failure to calculate the importance of religious perspectives arguably was a hindrance most of all to the loser of that election, Sen. John Kerry of Massachusetts, a Democrat and Roman Catholic. He came under scrutiny during the election from Steven Waldman, the editor of BeliefNet, and others, for the appearance of religion-avoidance.[13]

In an interview with reporters from the *Boston Globe* after the election, Kerry reflected on how religion in public life went beyond single-issue politics, and was worthy of more attention. He had lost to Bush among Catholic voters, who represent a broader segment of the voting population than just religious conservatives. He referred to ". . . the whole cloth of Catholicism, the whole cloth of responsibility, the solidarity of people to their community and to each other and ultimately to the Lord . . . I'll tell you—that teaching has always been inclusive of just wars, the environment, poverty, justice, social justice, and never been reduced to one point or another."[14]

For the press, those mainstream voters were also mainstream readers and viewers, and invited attention as well. News outlets had taken laudable steps to increase religion coverage in recent years, but old complaints remained: that such coverage was too compartmentalized in "religion news" and that the regular news report focused too much on the far right and secular left in politics and policy.

There were a number of reasons why the press wasn't getting it quite right. These ranged from conventional and familiar laments about why the press isn't doing a better job on everything it did to more subtle challenges in writing about policies and politics that are informed by religious attitudes and beliefs. But the most important reason may be the complexity of the way in which moral and religious centrists go about making decisions.

We often hear of individual politicians and members of the flock who are at odds with the teachings of their religious leaders. In some instances they have been criticized for behaving in a "cafeteria" style, selecting only those items of faith that were easiest for them to accept. In individual cases, there of course may be instances where people act in ways that are self-serving rather than hewing to the harder road of self-sacrifice called for by their faiths' teachings. However, this is a simplistic view of the American religious and political perspectives, especially today, and the press should be careful not to confuse self-serving cynicism with real values-based independence.

Because they share a set of common civic ideals and objectives with people of many backgrounds, religious Americans, and also those who are agnostic but moral, are shaped profoundly by a tradition of individualism and accommodation. This makes it possible for them to mix pragmatism and idealism when the teachings of their denominations or sects come in conflict with societal trends. It would be a mistake for reporters and editors to lose sight of this in trying to understand how people apply faith to their attitudes and participation in civics and politics.

Part of what may be going on is that Americans are informed by, and act on, parallel tracks of normative values. There are those derived from religion and those gleaned from education and common civic experience in a diverse society. They may belong to a church or party, but they are motivated as well by a streak of good old-fashioned American individualism. Their voting independence and unpredictability may be as attributable to a process of considered choice as to the "anger" the press finds in groups like the "tea party" activists, who drew renewed vigor from the Brown campaign.[15]

For example, if a person's religion regards homosexuality as sinful, the encounters he or she has in neighborhoods, schools, and work settings may produce a more accepting view, and hence a conflict in value systems. In some cases, this conflict gets resolved in favor of following church doctrine. However, the power of shared American values gives the religious individual a separate justification for an alternative.

Also as more religious ideas and perspectives become available, people who describe themselves as religious or spiritual may make their own pragmatic decisions from a menu of differing religious insights about what is right. Remember also that just because somebody is "unchurched" or in the "nones" category of the social scientists, it does not necessarily follow that they also are lacking a spiritual compass. They may just not like the politics of their parents' pastor, or they may disagree with church doctrine, or be in a relationship with somebody who comes out of a different tradition that keeps both parties out of church.[16] The press would do well to build some of these possibilities into its reporting and analysis.

What is true of individuals is true also of groups. To survive as a credible political and religious force in the diverse currents of 21st-century America, it is necessary to develop a level of skill at working with other points of view, or at least to maneuver around differences considered non-negotiable. As far back as the 1996 Republican

National Convention, Ralph Reed, at the time the executive director of the powerful Christian Coalition, reportedly encouraged a behind-the-scenes effort to find compromise platform language on abortion.[17] Since that time, there has been more conflict over social agendas, but some religious conservatives such as Pastor Rick Warren of Saddleback Church have identified a need for pragmatism—or at least priority-setting—in order to pursue larger objectives, and to survive in the marketplace of political and religious ideas.

Interestingly, the inability to be flexible and find common ground has been identified by the Harvard University religion professor Harvey Cox as part of the long-term viability problem built into the DNA of religious fundamentalists.[18] He has written that Protestant fundamentalism in the United States and Muslim fundamentalism around the world are declining in influence and doomed because of their selectivity of viewpoints, their unwillingness to compromise, and their inherent divisiveness. He writes, "The fundamentalist world view is unbending and monochrome, but today's world is variable and multi-hued, and the plurality is more and more visible."

The unbending perspective is precisely the opposite from that found in America's religious and moral center. Cox sees the trend to accommodation extending beyond the nation's borders. He identifies a change on the world's religious stage where people increasingly are deciding for themselves how to encounter religion, being "suspicious of the scaffolding, the doctrines, and hierarchies through which it has been conveyed."

In making their own religious choices, and in making political decisions or adopting their own personal views of a complex social issue, many faith-based Americans may choose the position that makes the most sense to them once they have considered all things. This can include an ordering of priorities such as the economy, health care, and the environment, along with however they may feel about abortion, the death penalty, gay marriage, or stem cell research. Or it can involve matching up competing personal values derived from one's religious doctrines on one side with allegiance to inculcated Western civic values. These include the importance of rule of law and democratic procedures, and belief in the need to make accommodation with others through fairness, toleration, and sense of justice. A voter operating from a faith basis may in effect consult an array of internalized priorities that in some instances may be in conflict with religious doctrine.

These religious centrists come nowadays from many religious traditions and belief systems, but have some shared values. As religious people, they have a generally positive outlook. Here we see why the faith-based center is so important in the competition over political and policy choices, and indeed, in the competition for the hearts and minds of people. It is, effectively, a kind of antidote to fundamentalism. In fact, it may be that this religious and political center is one tonic to sustain the entire American experiment, to keep it afloat and somehow renewable in the face of hostile ideologies and depressing news about the environment and the economic system.

If religious Americans are becoming comfortable with other faiths and even borrowing some of their ideas, it isn't a great leap to consider they will do their own thinking on social issues where denominations take different positions. In the area of bioethics, for example, the Roman Catholics and evangelicals have lined up in opposition to embryonic stem cell research, but the mainline Protestant churches and Jewish groups favor it for its potential to provide new medical advances. The death penalty and gay marriage have elicited very different views from religious groups.[19]

Motivated by faith, but instructed by an inner compass of civic values and experience living in a modern democracy, the moral and religious centrists follow their heads and hearts at the same time. They match up priorities to reach personal decisions that may not always be in lockstep or predictable. Add to this the agnostics and humanists who also are guided by moral considerations, but who may be put off by aspects of organized religion or the posturing of TV evangelists. Regardless of these people's views on the existence of God, they constitute values-based constituencies across a wide segment of the population.[20]

The question is, can the press step back and build an understanding of this into its reporting and analysis? It may not be possible to do this on every story, but certainly it can be done in trying to make sense of the big picture. By "big picture," I mean nothing less than the comprehensive reporting undertaken to understand and explain the public's national priorities arising out of core beliefs and attitudes. Tim Kelly in Chapter 11 will explain how conservative Christians, consisting of evangelicals and fundamentalists, became so important that they ended up constituting the very base of the Republican Party, which is a pretty big story. The lessons of the 2004 presidential election and some other things we've discussed suggest that faith-based considerations are there in assessing the priorities of all voters, not just those normally thought of as the religious right.

The question is how to do it. One way might be to consider that already, as a remedy for shortsighted coverage of national trends, some of the press's thoughtful members began to talk in recent years about a new kind of journalism that provided connections, not necessarily on stories involving religion but on those that required some context.

Writers like Ronald Brownstein of the National Journal and formerly the *Los Angeles Times* have exemplified the practice of this journalistic form by writing political pieces that were both timely and comprehensive in their reach. He told *Columbia Journalism Review* that he was endeavoring "to build a box around the information—some kind of conceptual framework."[21]

The result was a kind of interdisciplinary journalism, weaving forgotten moments from American political history into the interpretation of current events, or borrowing from sociologists or philosophers to explain the ramifications of policy. This approach would be a good tool for identifying religious impulses in the attitudes of Americans on controversial issues like abortion or gay marriage, or understanding how it is possible to be an evangelical and environmentalist, or discerning the influence of faith on all sorts of voting behavior or trends.

Unfortunately, there is too little of it, even in our best daily journals. For the most part, conceptual journalism remains most easily recognizable in longer forms of writing, such as can be found in publications like *the New Yorker* or *the Atlantic Monthly*. It will be a challenge to find ways to do this kind of reporting in the digital age, where budgets for traditional print-based and longer-form journalism are in short supply. The foundations and universities that have made worthy commitments in this area can help, and new online platforms may provide new kinds of outlet.

News organizations have a formidable task in explaining how religion informs day-to-day political attitudes and behavior of citizens and readers. While adept at delivering the results of polls in news reports, the press in the print and broadcast heyday was not adept at integrating these data into its reporting on how religious attitudes and perspectives shape politics, policy, and voting behavior.

It will take conscious effort to be aware that religious and moral sensibilities are important not only to the shrill Americans, but to the quiet ones. Moreover, to identify the true religious nature of the population requires spending time scanning an array of survey research.

It is easy for reporters to find religious conservatives who wear their positions on their sleeves. The secular left is not shy about voicing its concerns about the separation of church and state. But middle-ground religious voters who can be found in both major parties, or who are independent, are harder to identify. They don't necessarily talk about how religion factors into their decision making; indeed, they may do their own internal computation without fanfare or much discussion, even with friends or co-workers. Some belong to denominations; others are spiritual but not necessarily churched. Some, as has been happening in the Roman Catholic Church for years, make their own decisions about things like reproductive choices.

To report well on religion in our diverse nation, the press has a challenging but fascinating task of figuring out how these people think and act. So the memo to journalists should say, "As you consider the religious right, as you think about the secular liberals, take note also of the center as a place where important battles over religion, politics and policy are decided."

SUGGESTED DISCUSSION QUESTIONS

1. What dynamics of religious voters did James Dobson's retirement reveal?

2. What are the main characteristics of the religious center that distinguish them from the traditional religious voters?

3. A better understanding of the American religious landscape would lead to more nuanced reporting of politics by the media. Discuss.

4. According to the author, what is the most important reason the press hasn't been getting it right in its coverage of American politics vis-à-vis religion?

5. Americans derive their normative values from two main sources. What are they and how does the author think they work to inform the opinions of people in the religious center?

ENDNOTES

1. "Will Dobson's Resignation Refocus the Christian Right?" in "On Faith" column, appearing in the *Washington Post* blog "Under God," David Waters, February 27, 2009.

2. The sociologist James Davison Hunter popularized this term in his 1991 publication *Culture Wars: The Struggle to Define America* (Basic Books).

3. For more on these two stories of local interfaith initiatives and the effects of tides of immigration, see *Hallowed Ground,* Plenum (1997), Stephen Burgard.

4. Jen'nan Read in Chapter 10 and Tim Kelly in Chapter 11 focus in on the composition of some of these centrists and moderates, and describe their coordinates within two important groups, Islamic immigrants, and conservative Christians.

5. "U.S. Religious Landscape Survey," Pew Forum on Religion & Public Life, summary of findings, pewforum.org.

6. "Many Americans Mix Multiple Faiths," The Pew Forum on Religion and Public Life, December 9, 2009.

7. "Let the Explaining Begin!," Howard Kurtz, washingtonpost.com, November 8, 2004. The observations reported by Kurtz, and the *Columbia Journalism Review* article by Paul Starobin mentioned later in this chapter, were cited in "Press Credibility and Faith-Based Politics," Stephen Burgard, Center for the Study of Democracy, UC Irvine, April 5, 2005.

8. See "Brown and His Church Don't Wear Religion on the Sleeve," Monica Brady-Myerov, wbur.org, February 2, 2010. It has a discussion (and audio link) about Scott Brown's religious affiliation with New England Chapel, one of four congregations in Massachusetts affiliated with Christian Reformed Church in North America, a denomination that's a member of the National Association of Evangelicals. Accessed from http://www.wbur.org/2010/02/02/scott-browns-church.

9. To follow the evolution of this debate, see three *Boston Globe* stories. "Coakley decries health care bill," Matt Viser, November 10, 2009; "Coakley accepts curb on abortion coverage," Lisa Wangsness, December 21, 2009; "Abortion takes stage in Senate race," Matt Viser, January 13, 2010.

10. "Obama Calls for 'Up or Down Vote' on Health Care Bill," Sheryl Gay Stolberg and Robert Pear, *New York Times,* March 4, 2010. National Public Radio's *Morning Edition* reported the same day on concerns of moderate Democrats in the House.

11. "Moral Values Cited as Defining Issue of the Election," Katherine Q. Seelye, *New York Times,* November 4, 2004. The polls were conducted by Edison Media Research of Somerville, NJ, and Mitofsky International of New York City for the National Election Pool. According to the *Times* account, the results were based on questionnaires filled out by 13,660 voters in 250 precincts nationally. Telephone interviews also were conducted with absentee and early voters.

12. "Let the Explaining Begin!" Howard Kurtz, washingtonpost.com, November 8, 2004.

13. For a good discussion of religion in the 2004 presidential election, see "Religion and the Presidential Vote," The Pew Research Center For People and the Press, December 6, 2004.

14. "Weighing defeat, Kerry sees lessons to guide future," interview with Peter S. Canellos, Nina J. Easton, Michael Kranish, and Susan Milligan, *Boston Globe,* February 6, 2005.

15. For a report on this independent streak in its extreme form, a movement that can be at odds with political parties, authority, and even itself, see "Unity is not their cup of tea," Kathleen Hennessey, *Los Angeles Times,* January 25, 2010, p. A1.

16. Harvard's Robert D. Putnam discussed fluidity in the American religious landscape in his Harry Eckstein Lecture at UC Irvine entitled, "American Grace: The Changing Role of Religion in America" February 26, 2010.

17. "What the Christian Right Was Really Trying to Say," Paul A. Gigot, "Potomac Watch," *Wall Street Journal,* February 17, 1995.

18. "Why Fundamentalism Will Fail," Harvey Cox, *Boston Globe,* November 8, 2009, p. K1.

19. "Issues," The Pew Forum on Religion and Public Life.

20. Researchers Robert D. Putnam and David Campbell have interesting findings on young Americans who are dropping out of religion, especially arising from conservative politics, but posit that this may be temporary pending a time when "religious entrepreneurs will rise to offer these young Americans the less politicized religion that they crave." *Social Capital Blog,* The Saguaro Seminar, Harvard Kennedy School. Accessed from http://socialcapital.wordpress.com/2009/05/13/young-americans-dropping-out-of-religion-other-american-grace-findings/.

21. "The Conceptual Scoop," Paul Starobin, *Columbia Journalism Review,* January/February 1996.

CHAPTER 10

The Diversity of the New Immigrant Religious Population

Jen'nan Ghazal Read

Covering religions such as Islam in the United States requires open-mindedness about the new religious terrain. Jen'nan Read, a Carnegie scholar based at Duke University and formerly at UC Irvine, has studied the diversity of the new Islamic population. In an age of ideological conflict between western values and religious perspectives, her findings can help journalists understand an important dimension of the domestic story of Islam.

The events of September 11, 2001, propelled Muslim-Americans into the media spotlight, a group that had gone largely unnoticed and unknown to the average American. In the years since of relatively intense media attention, there continues to be widespread confusion in distinguishing national, ethnic, and religious diversity among Muslim-Americans and a general tendency to conflate Arab ethnicity with Muslim religion and Muslim religion with Islamic fundamentalism. Indeed, recent nationwide polls conducted by the Pew Research Center show that most Americans consider Islam a threat to democracy, both globally and locally, and by extension most Americans fear that Muslims cannot be integrated into the democratic fabric of American life.[1] Moreover, most think that Islam is very different from their own religion and consider Muslims as outside the American mainstream.

But how real is this perceived threat? Do Muslim-Americans differ from other Americans in terms of their values, beliefs, attitudes, and behaviors? Do they differ from each other based on racial/ethnic group membership? And what dimensions of religious identity, if any, influence Muslim-American political participation? In other words, what about being Muslim matters for political involvement and how does this differ from other Americans? The questions are significant for all Americans, but they are especially important for reporters, editors, and producers who act as mediators between newsmakers and consumers of news.

In this chapter, I use national survey data on Muslim-Americans and multiple national-level data sources on the American public to examine these pressing questions. After defining the demographic make-up of the Muslim-American population, I turn to their attitudes and beliefs, with an eye toward comparing them with other American ethnic and religious groups. I then focus more specifically on the role and participation of Muslims in American politics as a way to shed light on future possibilities for understanding the assimilation of this group. The hope is to help journalists better understand Muslim-Americans so that their reporting will be more informed and accurate.

Who Are Muslims in America?

A common concern in the American discourse on Muslim integration is whether or not Islam is antithetical to democracy and democratic participation. Fueling this concern is the widespread misconception that Muslim-Americans are a homogeneous population comprised primarily of Arabs whose loyalties are divided between the United States and Middle East. Recent nationwide polls by the Pew Research Center found that 42 percent of Americans think that the majority of Muslims around the world are anti-American, 36 percent have an unfavorable opinion of Islam, and 35 percent feel that Islam is more likely than other religions to encourage violence, even though 66 percent admit that they know very little or nothing about the religion.[2]

This confusion stems in part from the vast diversity that characterizes Muslims abroad and in the United States and the tendency to collapse both groups into one homogenous category. A good place to start undoing this confusion is by defining who they are, both globally and locally. Globally, Islam is the largest and fastest growing faith tradition in the world, with one out of five people belonging to the Islamic religion. South Asia is home to the largest Muslim nations, with 215 million Muslims in Indonesia (88 percent of the country's population) and another 160 million in Pakistan (97 percent of the country's population). Predominately Muslim populations are also located in North Africa and Western Asia, including in Egypt, Algeria, Morocco, and Tunisia (North Africa) and Syria, Iraq, Iran, and Jordan (Western Asia). While many of these countries are Arab, the majority of Muslims globally are of non-Arab ethnicity, including Pakistanis, Indians, and Persians.

This diversity is reflected in the Muslim population in the United States, which is the most ethnically diverse Muslim population in the world originating from over 80 countries around the globe. Size estimates of the U.S. Muslim population are contentious, ranging anywhere from 2 to 8 million. Due to the constitutional separation of church and state, the U.S. Census Bureau does not collect information on religion, thus official counts of Muslim-Americans are nonexistent. Scholarly studies conducted by Muslim sociologists in the late 1990s projected that the population would number around 7 million by 2000, an estimate that was later revised to 5.7 million in 2003.[3] Similarly, the 2001 Mosque Study Project placed the Muslim-American population at 6 to 7 million.[4] In contrast, a 2001 study sponsored by the American Jewish Committee put the number much lower at 1.9 to 2.8 million.[5] A plausible estimate comes from the CIA World Factbook and places the population at 1 percent of the U.S. population,[6] or roughly 3 million persons.

Although there is considerable debate over the size of the population, there is more agreement among scholars on the social and demographic composition of the community. About two-thirds of Muslims are indigenous to the Middle East, South Asia, and Africa; one-third of the population is African-American; and a small but growing number are U.S.-born Anglo and Hispanic converts to the religion. The vast majority of the indigenous population is immigrant, and most have resided in the United States for ten or more years (i.e., they are not new arrivals). Muslim immigration to the United States reached its peak in the 1970s and 1980s, and has been relatively slow over the past ten years due to restrictive immigration policies passed in the 1990s, namely the 1996 Illegal Immigration and Reform Act. Although most of the indigenous population is foreign-born, an increasing number is second- and third-generation offspring of earlier immigrant arrivals. The indigenous population is further diverse by ethnicity, with South Asians (30 to 35 percent) and Arabs (20 to 25 percent) making up the two largest ethnic groups.

A sizeable and growing percentage of the population is comprised of U.S.-born black Americans, or African-Americans. African-American Muslims differ from the indigenous population in several ways, most notably being that they are typically converts to the religion. Most African-American converts to Islam today adhere to mainstream Islam (Sunni or Shia), similar to the indigenous population. Mainstream, or orthodox, Islam can be thought of as referring to those branches of Islam that are rooted in the fundamental philosophies of the Islamic religion as laid out in the Koran and hadiths, which are second-hand reports of the Prophet Muhammed's personal traditions and lifestyle that detail how he dealt with daily issues and problems. In addition to adherents of mainstream Islam, a large number of African-American Muslims belong to the Nation of Islam, which was established in 1930 by Wallace Fard Muhammad, and is considered a more politically-oriented branch of Islam.

Muslim-Americans tend to be highly educated and fluent in English, reflecting the selective nature of immigration and restrictive immigration policies that limit who gains admission into the United States. On average, they share similar socio-economic characteristics with the general U.S. population: one-fourth has a bachelor's degree or higher, one-fourth lives in households with incomes of $75,000/year or more, and the majority are employed.[7] But not all Muslims share these average traits—some are living in poverty with poor English language skills and few resources needed to improve their situation.

One of the most important and overlooked facts about Muslim-Americans is that they are not uniformly religious and devout. Some are religiously devout, some are religiously moderate, and some are non-practicing and secular, basically Muslim in name only, similar to a good proportion of U.S. Christians and Jews. Some attend a mosque on a weekly basis and pray every day, and others don't engage in either practice. Even among the more religiously devout, there is still a sharp distinction between being a good Muslim and being an Islamic fundamentalist. Indeed, many Muslim-Americans emigrated from countries in the Middle East that are now targeted in the war on terror, in part to practice their religion and politics more freely in the United States.

Muslim-American Values and Politics

Contrary to popular belief, evidence from the Pew Research Center, General Social Survey, and Project MAPS (Muslim-Americans in the Public Square) all point to a group that looks much more like mainstream America than popular stereotypes imply. On social issues, family life, and domestic policies, Muslim-Americans look very similar to other American groups. On hot-button issues like abortion, they actually fall in line with the views of evangelical Christians.

Perhaps not surprisingly, Muslim-Americans are slightly more critical of U.S. foreign policies in the Middle East, in part due to the fact that many have roots in these parts of the world. Their attitudes vary by racial and ethnic group membership, with African-American Muslims expressing more grievances about the treatment of Muslims in American society and being more critical of American politics than South Asian and Arab Muslims, in part reflecting their long-standing racialized position.

How do these values translate into political action (i.e., democratic participation), if they do at all? I have suggested that Muslim-Americans have the characteristics to be active participants in American democracy (e.g., well-educated), but do they participate, and if so, where do they fit? Prior to September 11, Muslim-Americans may have been politically active, but they typically mobilized based on individualized interests like many other Americans (localized concerns over the economy, health care, education, etc.). Things changed on that day. The events and ensuing months and years have propelled Muslims into the spotlight of American public discourse and debate. The events of that day also served to heighten Muslim-American political consciousness, which has facilitated mobilization efforts by Muslim-American organizations to increase their participation in the political process. Further, the ongoing wars in Iraq and against terrorism, interpreted by some Muslim-Americans as a war against Islam (both radical and mainstream Islam), have ensured that Muslim advocacy groups have an active and vocal base.

In 2004, the Council on American-Islamic Relations (CAIR) worked diligently to get out the Muslim vote, especially in key battleground states such as Ohio, Florida, and California. Their efforts included opening "Get Out the Muslim Vote" election centers throughout Ohio, calling thousands of Ohio and Florida Muslim voters to ask for a commitment to vote, bussing Florida Muslim voters to early polls after Friday prayers, and publishing a voter guide for Muslim voters in California.

These efforts resulted in the unprecedented, successful mobilization of Muslim-American voters: In 2004, a record high number of Muslim-Americans were elected to public office — nearly 50 percent of the 100 candidates nationwide — and there was a dramatic shift away from President Bush, with only 7 percent of Muslim-American voters supporting his candidacy, down from over 40 percent in 2000. In 2008, we witnessed an even higher turnout of Muslim-American voters, though the actual numbers are unknown. The vast majority voted for Barack Obama, again signaling their distrust of the past two administration's policies toward Muslims in the United States and abroad.

Overall then, Muslim-American political involvement is influenced by similar factors that influence your average American. Muslim-Americans who are more educated, have higher incomes, higher levels of group consciousness, and who feel more marginalized from mainstream society (i.e., discrimination) are more politically active than are those without these characteristics. Similar to other Americans, these are individuals who feel that they have more at stake in political outcomes, and thus are more motivated to try and influence such outcomes.

Perhaps most importantly, Muslim religious identity is not uniformly associated with political engagement. Similar to U.S. Christians, the personal dimensions of Muslim identity — or being a devout Muslim — have little influence on their political involvement, while the more organizational and political dimensions provide a collective identity that stimulates Muslim-American political activity. Rather than interpret this as bolstering stereotypes that link Islamic worship with political incitement, I argue that mosques provide environments that are similar to other congregations in that they serve to heighten group consciousness and awareness of issues that need to be addressed through political mobilization, such as policies to remedy discrimination.

These findings track closely with what is known about the religion-politics connection among other U.S. ethnic and religious groups, such as evangelical Christians and African-Americans, and suggest that the Muslim experience is less distinct than popular beliefs imply. These findings also provide new insight into the religion-politics connection by showing how different dimensions of religious identity (personal, organizational, and political) influence both the degree and direction of involvement in American politics.

The take-home message for the media is that stories that compare Muslims to other American groups may shed greater insight into their experiences than single-focused ones that result in highlighting what is different or unusual about them. In other words, there may be much to learn about Muslims by situating their beliefs, attitudes, and behaviors in relation to those of other Americans.

Conclusion

I began the chapter by highlighting the confusion that remains rampant regarding Muslims in America, particularly among average Americans. But the news is not all bad. There has been a growing level of sophistication and understanding from reporters and journalists regarding Muslim beliefs and practices and how Muslim-Americans fit into the national landscape. Compared with just a few years ago, the questions I received during Ramadan recently revolved much less around stereotypes of Muslims as oppressors of women who are violent, singularly focused, and irrational and more around the civic and religious engagement of Muslims relative to other American groups. Some of the most informed questions came from journalists who had direct contact with Muslims in their communities — they had greater insight into the complexities of the Muslim population and to the similarities that they shared with others.

This leads me to believe that the press's overall coverage of Muslims in America will continue to improve as their levels of exposure and interaction with them increases. As a sociologist, I know that one of the most effective methods for overcoming stereotypes is through social interaction. In other words, it is much harder to apply a generalized image when that image does not resonate with personal experience. Thus, for the same reason that I am encouraged about more informed news coverage in the United States, I am concerned about the quality of coverage on Muslims abroad as more and more media outlets are closing shop in the Middle East (and elsewhere).

SUGGESTED DISCUSSION QUESTIONS

1. Why do most Americans consider Islam a threat to democracy and thus fear that Muslims cannot be integrated into the democratic fabric of American life? Is this threat real according to the findings cited in this chapter?

2. In what ways have the events of September 11, 2001, and ensuing months and years propelled Muslims into the spotlight of American public discourse and debate?

3. Explain how Muslim-American political involvement is influenced by similar factors that influence average Americans.

4. What significance can be drawn from the author's conclusion that Muslim-Americans look much more like mainstream Americans than the stereotypes suggest?

5. What does the author think can make for better coverage of Muslim-Americans in the future and how than this come about?

ENDNOTES

1. The Pew Research Center for the People & the Press, *Plurality Sees Islam as More Likely to Encourage Violence: Views of Islam Remain Sharply Divided,* accessed from http://pewforum.org/publications/surveys/islam.pdf, September 9, 2004.

2. Ibid.

3. Philippa Strum and Danielle Tarantolo, Eds., *Muslims in the United States: Demography, Beliefs, Institutions; Proceedings of a conference sponsored by the Division of United States Studies, Woodrow Wilson International Center for Scholars,* June 18, 2003.

4. Ihsan Bagby, et al., *The Mosque in America: A National Portrait,* A Report from the Mosque Study Project, April 26, 2001.

5. Tom W. Smith, *Estimating the Muslim Population in the United States,* American Jewish Committee, accessed from http://www.ajc.org/site/apps/nl/content3.asp?c= ijITI2PHKoG&b=843637&ct=1044159.

6. https://www.cia.gov/library/publications/the-world-factbook/geos/us.html.

7. Jeanna Bryner, *The Truth About Muslims in America,* October 30, 2008, accessed from http://www.livescience.com/culture/081030-muslim-americans.html.

CHAPTER 11

Understanding the Christian Right and the 'New' Evangelicals

Timothy A. Kelly

Timothy A. Kelly goes beyond stereotypes and misconceptions to explain who's who in some important groups of conservative Christians. He also provides tools for journalists to use in understanding their various perspectives. He is director of TAK Consult, and until recently directed the DePree Public Policy Institute at Fuller Theological Seminary in Pasadena, CA. He is a former Virginia state mental health commissioner, and has taught at several major universities, including Vanderbilt University, where he also received his doctorate. He served as associate professor of psychology at the Fuller Graduate School of Psychology from 2008–2009.

"Followers of the 'Christian right,' are 'largely poor, uneducated, and easy to command.'"[1]

"The notion that Christianity in general and Evangelicalism in particular are by nature right-wing creeds has always been wrong. How can a faith built around a commitment to the poor and the vulnerable be seen as leading ineluctably to conservative political conclusions?"[2]

Based on these quotes, one might say that the *Washington Post* did a turnaround over the past 15 years—from disdain to appreciation for conservative Christianity. In 1993, the common view among many reporters and commentators was that the devout simply obey, sheep-like, whatever their preferred religious leaders ask them to do. And usually, that was to support conservative causes (e.g., opposing abortion and same-sex marriage) and vote Republican. The general perception in many newsrooms was of Neanderthal-like fundamentalists who held rigidly to outdated notions of morality, and who were attempting to force their limiting views on the rest of society.

But times have changed, and many in the media are now becoming more interested in issues of faith and values as legitimate expression of human concerns in a pluralistic, democratic society. For instance, since 2001 *National Public Radio (NPR)* has run a popular series titled *Speaking of Faith,* which focuses on "the intersection of theology and human experience, of grand religious ideas and real life."[3] Since 2006, *Newsweek* and the *Washington Post* have sponsored a blog called *On Faith,* noting that "Religion is the most pervasive yet least understood topic in global life."[4]

Such interest goes all the way up to the White House, which has discovered that issues of faith are legitimately relevant to public policy. Since 2001 there has been an office dedicated to faith-based issues — currently titled the "White House Office of Faith-Based and Neighborhood Partnerships." In dedicating the office, President Obama stated:

> "[C]hange that Americans are looking for will not come from government alone. There is a force for good greater than government. It is an expression of faith, this yearning to give back, this hungering for a purpose larger than our own."[5]

Of course, the kind of faith referred to by *NPR, Newsweek,* the *Washington Post* or the White House is very broad, and includes not only organized religion but also personal spirituality that could mean simply feeling a sense of oneness with the universe. A full 85 percent of Americans report that religion is "fairly or very important"[6] in their lives, but what does this really mean? More importantly for students of journalism, political science, and related fields — how can one understand and report on the role of faith in both the personal and public spheres of life, when faith can be such a vague and confusing topic?

There are many kinds of faith in our pluralistic society, but one in particular seems to have captured the imagination of the media over the past 20 years or so — that of the "Christian right" (or "religious right"). All faiths are relevant to the issues of the day, since all teach specific principles and values that relate to human behavior and social structures. A Jewish person is no more or less concerned for issues of human rights or environmentalism, for instance, than is a Muslim or a Christian. All may well find that their faith directly informs their political beliefs, how they live in society, and how they vote.

Nonetheless, the Christian right has been singled out as the most potent religious voting block in the nation, and thus a force to be reckoned with. There is some warrant for this, given the track record of two political organizations that grew out of the Christian right: the Moral Majority in the 1980s (widely credited with the 1984 re-election of President Reagan), and the Christian Coalition in the 1990s (a more sophisticated organization that grew out of the Moral Majority). But what do we know about those who constitute the Christian right, usually referred to as "fundamentalists" and "evangelicals"? Furthermore, what about the "new" evangelicals—who are they and how do they differ? How can journalists, political scientists, and others understand these groups and report accurately on their respective beliefs and actions?

These are the questions that this chapter seeks to address. In doing so, the concept of "principled centrism" is put forward as a means for understanding what differentiates today's "new" evangelicals from fundamentalists and traditional evangelicals. But first, we must define key terms.

Terms of Faith

When speaking on matters of religion, it is very easy to miscommunicate. People of faith have very precise definitions of their religious terms that are often not well understood by those reporting on or researching the group. It is thus incumbent upon the researcher to make sure that key terms are defined carefully and grasped fully before proceeding. Otherwise, conclusions drawn may be superficial or even altogether invalid. For instance, there is a great deal of difference between what a Catholic Christian means by saying, "I belong to the Catholic church" (i.e., referring to the Roman Catholic Church headed by the pope), and what a Protestant Christian means when saying, "I belong to the worldwide catholic church" (i.e., referring to all professing Christians regardless of denomination). To say that they both see themselves as "belonging to the Catholic church," without clarifying the difference, would be confusing to all parties. Accordingly, following are definitions for the terms of this discussion.

There are two key terms that always must be addressed when reporting on anything to do with faith: "religion" and "spirituality." Religion is typically seen as related to more formalized approaches to seeking God involving established theological teachings, traditional practices, denominations, and places of worship. However, there is no precise definition of religion with which all theologians would agree. Instead, I offer a dictionary definition that is generic enough to reflect a pluralistic approach, yet specific enough to be meaningful:

Religion: belief in a divine power to be worshipped and obeyed as the creator and ruler of the universe, expressed in conduct and ritual.[7]

"Spirituality" too is a word with many meanings—often used to refer to a more subjective, psychologically-oriented, less formalized approach to seeking God. A person can be spiritual without being religious, and this may be seen as more authentic than following the directives of a church, synagogue, or mosque.

Spirituality: the individual's personal, subjective expression of their search for transcendent meaning and purpose, which may or may not involve organized religion.[8]

Although some see religion and spirituality as unrelated, it is perhaps best to see them as two sides of one coin. A religious person who lacks spirituality may be seen as superficial, and a spiritual person who is anti-religion may be seen as self-indulgent. In contrast, a person who is both spiritual and religious can be seen as demonstrating a credible maturity of faith and practice — responsibly engaged in organized religion but also personally committed to the practice of spirituality.

Not surprisingly, most fundamentalists, evangelicals, and "new" evangelicals would claim to be both religious and spiritual, because they attend church but go far beyond that in their daily life of faith.

But just what is a "new" evangelical, and is such a person part of the Christian right or something else altogether? Although there are many ways to answer this question, I would like to suggest that the Christian right consists of two well-established sub-groups, fundamentalists and evangelicals,[9] whereas the "new" evangelicals (or "neo-evangelicals") represent an altogether new phenomenon, what I call "the Principled Center." These three subgroups are often lumped together in the media as the Christian right. But this is confusing and inaccurate because it ignores significant differences between fundamentalists and evangelicals, and even more importantly because it misses the point that the "new" evangelicals are altogether distinct from the Christian right.

Fundamentalism is a highly charged word, often applied to extremists in any religious or ideological camp. Thus it is possible to be a fundamentalist Christian, Muslim, environmentalist, or even atheist! The inferred meaning is that such a person holds rigidly and harshly to a core set of beliefs, and will not engage in the usual give-and-take of civil dialogue with those who do not hold such views. Their actions are seen as extreme and potentially dangerous, whether that be threatening a doctor who performs abortions, supporting Islamic terrorism, vandalizing car dealerships that sell gas-guzzlers, or torching churches. In each case, the most troubling part is that the person committing the violence is convinced that he or she is doing the right thing.

Fundamentalism originally had a much more benign meaning. It was coined in the early 20th century to refer to conservative Christians who held to a set of fundamental theological beliefs, in contrast to more liberal Christians. Accordingly, fundamentalists were those who believed in the divinity of Christ, the authority of the Bible, miracles, the atonement of Christ for sin, and the coming return of Christ — tenets laid out in a series of books published in the early 1900s entitled *The Fundamentals: A Testimony to the Truth*.[10]

Unfortunately, over time the fundamentalist movement became anti-intellectual, socially rigid, and distrustful of society — with a tendency toward separatism. In response, well-known conservative Christian leaders[11] began distinguishing evangelicalism from fundamentalism. Prior to this time the two terms had been used more or less synonymously. But from the 1940s on, evangelicalism came to stand for pursuing Ivy-League-level conservative theological scholarship, engaging social justice issues, and cooperating with society and the broader church in order to promote renewal—both social and spiritual. The difference between fundamentalism and evangelicalism thus is not primarily theological.

First, here's what they have in common. Both groups hold to three core theological beliefs:

- Biblical authority. The authority of scripture is recognized as relevant not only to theological beliefs but also to daily life practices.

- Christ's sacrifice for sin. The central message of Christianity revolves around the belief that Jesus Christ died on the cross for humanity's sins, and can be "accepted" as personal savior.

- Conversion of nonbelievers. It is important to tell others about Jesus Christ so that they too may have opportunity to repent and have their sins forgiven, live a godly life, and be heaven-bound.

However, the two groups differ markedly in how they respond to society. Fundamentalists tend to have a separatist mentality toward secular thought and culture, which can lead to a rigid, harsh, isolationist stance that permeates both thinking and lifestyle. The definition of fundamentalism in its current usage must therefore include both its attitude toward core beliefs and its social reactivity:

Fundamentalism: Reducing a religion or ideology to its basic tenets, strictly and rigidly held, while rejecting modern social norms and political life as doctrinally threatening.

But here is a critical point that is often missed by outsiders reporting on the Christian right. It is definitely possible to hold onto the three core Christian theological beliefs listed above and *not be* a fundamentalist. In contrast to the fundamentalist, the evangelical Christian is comfortable in academe, in the marketplace of current ideas, and in modern social settings. Whereas the fundamentalist may seem out of touch with the times, the evangelical is socially and politically savvy. The best-known formal definition of evangelicalism[12] thus adds a fourth component to the tripartite theology of Biblical authority, Christ's sacrifice, and need for conversion.

It is the social activism component that differentiates the evangelical from the fundamentalist—the desire to engage the world fully, to be active in society in a relevant and effective manner, including in the political arena. Accordingly, the definition of evangelical must incorporate not only theological beliefs, but also social activism.

Evangelicalism: Holding to the traditional conservative Christian beliefs of Biblical authority, Christ's sacrifice and need for conversion, while actively engaging modern society so as to improve the quality of life for all.

It is not surprising that much dialogue and contention exists between these conservative Christian perspectives. The fundamentalist distrusts society (and evangelicals) and prefers to keep his or her distance. The evangelical intends to improve, or even "redeem," society through social activism. Both hold to the tripartite theological beliefs listed above, but they differ markedly in the application of theology to society and the issues of the day.

The Rise of the Christian Right

It is beyond the scope of this chapter to document the historical and theological course of fundamentalism and evangelicalism, especially since other texts have done so superbly. However, at the risk of over-simplifying, it is important to note in broad brush strokes something about how these two groups developed through the latter half of the 20th century. Fundamentalism and evangelicalism sometimes had bitter theological fights throughout the 1950s, 1960s, and 1970s (e.g., over whether or not to engage society, the meaning of Biblical inerrancy, the role of women in the church, etc.).

The social activism of the evangelical perspective had not yet blossomed, and the isolationism of the fundamentalist perspective held sway. Then in the 1980s something unexpected happened. A conservative pastor from Virginia, Jerry Falwell, founded the Moral Majority and succeeded in convincing fundamentalists and evangelicals alike to engage the political process. Prior to this time, most conservative Christians either held that their religious beliefs did not apply to the storm and stress of politics and policy (fundamentalism), or did not see any meaningful way to engage the issues of the day (frustrated evangelicalism).

It is hard to overstate the political significance of this shift, which continued in the form of Pat Robertson's Christian Coalition during the 1990s. For over two decades the Moral Majority and Christian Coalition provided a structure within which conservative Christians could become involved in the political process, especially at the national level of presidential and congressional elections. Their core concerns were over the perceived assault on faith and family values via abortion-on-demand, same-sex marriage, premarital sex, value-free education, and the "naked public square" that seemingly had no room for people of faith to have their voices heard.[13]

Thus in the 1980s and 1990s conservative Christians found a mechanism for pursuing the social activism that evangelicals had begun calling for. Some fundamentalists refused to participate, but others overcame their preference for isolation in the hope of stemming the growing tide of immorality they perceived around them. They begrudgingly supported the effort, and this development overall was so profound that for a time it moved some fundamentalists from one definition of conservative Christianity into the other—into the "evangelical" frame of mind. On the other hand, the evangelicals finally found their activist voice and engaged the political arena with growing confidence and sophistication.

Amazingly, this entire group quickly became potent enough to be considered the base of the Republican Party. Republicans who appealed to the Christian right were considered to be in safe territory politically. Those who ignored the base did so at their own peril. Eventually, the Christian right came to be seen as simply one component of the Republican Party—concerned primarily about abortion and same-sex marriage, and capable of turning out voters in amazing numbers. Evangelical pastors even handed out voter guides to their congregations to inform their parishioners of candidates' voting records before an election, a practice that drew several court challenges regarding separation of church and state.

One might question whether or not it is in the best interest of the Christian right to identify so closely with the Republican Party, just as one might question whether it is in the best interest of the African-American community to identify so closely with the Democratic Party. In both cases, the risk is that the party eventually will take the constituency for granted, since they have nowhere else to go. What happens, then, when the constituency has concerns that are not well addressed by their given party— say a pro-life African-American or an environmentalist evangelical? Marching in lockstep with the party gives power to the party's overall political agenda, but what if that agenda fails to take into account some of their constituents' heartfelt concerns?

Questions like these are leading many voters to reconsider traditional party allegiance, as well as commitment to the left or right of the political spectrum, and look instead at the concept of political centrism.[14] For example, a *Wall Street Journal* poll run a few weeks before the 2008 presidential election found that 43 percent of the undecided swing voters called themselves independents, and 47 percent saw themselves as centrists.[15]

The 'New' Evangelicals and Principled Centrism

This movement toward the center has fractured the Christian right, as increasing numbers drop out of their lockstep march with political conservatism in general and the Republican Party in particular. After all, what to do if as an evangelical you are concerned about high abortion rates but also environmental challenges? What if you support fiscal conservatism and small government but also some forms of social progressivism? Is it possible to be patriotic and strongly support national security, and yet also care deeply about homelessness and poverty? What if you're simply fed up with the polarizing rancor coming from both parties, from the far right and the far left, and you long for a third alternative?

These are the questions that have motivated a large number of evangelicals to disassociate themselves from Christian right and reconsider party allegiance as well as conservative/liberal identification. On a national level, the Christian right still packs a wallop, as shown by exit polls following the 2008 presidential election. According to the Barna Group,[16] 61 percent of the evangelical vote went to McCain versus 38 percent for Obama.[17]

But there is another story that comes to light when analyzing election "late-deciders," as well as battleground states where the Obama campaign specifically reached out to evangelicals. A Time/CNN poll found that evangelical late-deciders split evenly between Obama and McCain. Also, they found that the evangelical vote was impacted greatly in battleground states that were engaged by the Obama campaign's "evangelical outreach coordinators." These operatives brought in Democrat-leaning evangelicals (e.g., the well-known Christian author Donald Miller) to make the case for Obama, with striking results. In Indiana, for example, the evangelical vote showed a 14-point gain for Obama when compared with evangelical support for Kerry in 2004.[18] There is hunger for new alternatives such as principled centrism, in place of the old paradigm of liberal-Democrat versus conservative-Republican.

Widespread yearning for a principled center helps explain the amazing success of the "new" evangelical pastor Rick Warren, author of *The Purpose-Driven Life* and head of Saddleback Church in Lake Forest, CA. In response to a question as to whether he is politically liberal or conservative, he responded "right wing—left wing—I'm for the whole bird."[19] Warren's political positions are as frustrating to the far left as they are to the far right. He is against same-sex marriage but for civil unions. He is pro-life but vigorously addresses issues of poverty and disease. He is as concerned about reducing AIDS and illiteracy as he is about improving national security. When Warren hosted the presidential candidates' debate at Saddleback in August 2008, he carefully stated that he considered both Barack Obama and John McCain to be personal friends. His selection by Obama to offer the inaugural prayer angered many on the left who disagreed with Warren's positions on homosexuality and abortion, as well as many on the right who saw him as "selling out" to the incoming Obama administration.

But this is exactly what it means to be in the principled center of the political spectrum. It means having core principles and values that set the parameters for policy positions, and applying them to the issues of the day without regard to partisan or ideological imperatives. Consequently, it often means taking heat from both the left and the right. Centrism alone means standing for little more than compromise. Principled centrism means standing for core issues regardless of whose ox gets gored. Centrism alone may come across as lacking in courage, conviction, and passion. In contrast, the principled centrist can be both passionate and courageous, but appeals to core principles rather than ruling parties or ideologies.

One benefit of principled centrism is that by definition it crosses divisive partisan boundaries. When Warren and Obama find that they are both passionate about reducing AIDS, or when Warren and McCain find that they are both passionate about reducing abortions, partnerships are created that defy partisan or ideological explanation. The result? Instead of vilifying those who are members of the opposing party, principled centrists tend to listen and dialogue in a civil manner. The goal is to understand those with whom one does not necessarily agree, based on an analysis of the underlying principles and values. Then, with that understanding, common ground may be sought. This is one of the hallmarks of "new" evangelicals.

For instance, both pro-choice and pro-life supporters agree that quality of life is an important human right (although they do not agree on whether or not a fetus has human rights before birth). The fundamentalist might argue that pro-choice politicians are to be resisted at all costs, and the traditional evangelical might argue that only 100 percent pro-life candidates should be supported. But the "new" evangelical would be open to dialoguing with policymakers who are not necessarily pro-life in order to seek common ground on the need to: reduce unwanted pregnancies, increase the care and comfort of women who carry to birth, and expand adoption programs.

Beyond Partisanship

What does all this mean? It means that reporters and social scientists must get beyond the sweeping generalities of terms such as the "Christian right" and "fundamentalists" and drill down to the level of the group or individual in question. The times they are a-changing, and the "new" evangelicals are not going to automatically hold to conservative policy positions and vote Republican. They will evaluate each policymaker and each issue through the lens of their core principles, and identify what fits within those parameters and what doesn't. They will function independently of party or ideology, though easily work with one or the other if there is a fit on a given issue at a given time. Instead of party loyalty, look for loyalty to core principles and values—a perspective that is healthier than partisan politics as usual and closer to what the founding fathers had in mind when they contemplated an informed, engaged, and independent electorate.

President Obama campaigned as a post-partisan candidate throughout the 2008 election cycle. It remains to be seen to what extent this may or may not be true, but it is very significant that such a claim was attractive to voters. The electorate is sick of politics as usual, including the two parties that control the political process in such a self-serving manner, often at the obvious expense of the public good. For this reason, now would probably be an opportune moment for the launching of an independent party. But forming a viable third party in the United States is a daunting challenge when so much of the political oxygen (read: funding) has been soaked up by the established parties. Perhaps what we are witnessing is the functional rise of a "third party" within the two-party structure, expressed in the form of principled centrists such as the "new" evangelicals. This could serve to break the stranglehold on policy and politics that the status quo parties have had for so long, yet without having to actually form a third party.

One example of post partisanship and the desire for a third party is the so-called "Tea Party" movement. It is difficult to classify the Tea Party since it is comprised of a disparate array of constituents who do not normally collaborate (e.g., libertarians, social conservatives, economic conservatives, centrist progressives). But if one thing is clear it is that the Tea Party does not feel beholden to either party, as evidenced by their strong stand against incumbents of both parties.

A Case in Point

One example of the "new" evangelical perspective comes from Fuller Theological Seminary, located in Pasadena, CA. Fuller is the world's largest accredited seminary, boasts three schools (theology, intercultural studies, and psychology), and is one of the leading evangelical Christian academies in the world. Fuller is known as an institute of higher learning that holds to the core tenets of evangelical Christianity, yet freely engages people and institutions of other faiths, or of no faith. For instance, there is on-going dialogue with Muslims, Mormons, and Jews, as well as with local government authorities, over issues of mutual concern. Fuller could thus also be seen as a leading institution for the "new" evangelical movement.

From 2007–2009, Fuller launched the DePree Public Policy Institute[20] in order to speak out more clearly on the issues of the day, and to advance the public good. This was the only public policy institute associated with a seminary, and it promoted the concept of principled centrism as a framework for public policy debate. For example, the institute published opinion editorials in newspapers and journal articles that addressed a current concern from a principled centrist perspective.[21]

Principled centrism focuses on finding solutions to problems, regardless of the political spectrum of the source, as long as the resultant policy fits within the parameters of the core principles being adhered to. Principled centrism could also be called principled pragmatism. The focus is on what works to make life better for all, but unlike pure pragmatism there are limits within which policies are to be created and implemented. Those limits are set by the core principles.

What are some examples of core principles? One set that is being developed by the author follows the acronym "decent":

- Diverse communities with thriving families
- Effective education for all
- Clean environment
- Economic growth (jobs)

- National security
- Tax relief (limited, efficient, and effective government)

These principles defy party classification since some are associated with the left and others with the right. Furthermore, they constitute but one example of a set of principles that are policy relevant. It is important to note that principled centrism does not mandate which specific principles must be followed — only that one's principles need to be honestly articulated so that common ground may be found and progress made.

Conclusion

The world of conservative Christian faith, including fundamentalists, evangelicals, and "new" evangelicals, is much more diverse and nuanced than most commentators have acknowledged. It is no more appropriate to confuse evangelicalism with fundamentalism than it is to confuse Ivy League universities with community colleges. To avoid this, reporters and researchers must do their due diligence and cover the areas detailed in this chapter. In doing so, there is a logical sequence that should be followed — moving from theological to social to political questions.

- *Theological Questions.* It is appropriate to ask people of the Christian faith whether or not they believe in Biblical authority, Christ's sacrifice for sin, and the conversion of non-believers (as defined above). If so, then they are indeed holding to traditional, conservative Christian theological beliefs. However, this is not enough to classify them as part of the Christian right. (If they do not endorse these three beliefs, then they likely hold to a more liberal theological perspective.)

- *Social Isolation Questions.* The theological questions should be followed up with social questions to determine whether or not the interviewees take a separatist approach toward society. If so, if they are isolated and distrustful of others, then they are likely in the fundamentalist wing of the Christian right. This group is shrinking by the day, and is numerically far smaller than the evangelical wing, but can be very vocal.

- *Social Engagement Questions.* If those being interviewed endorse the traditional theological statements and are not separatist but instead engage with society and attempt to promote the public good, then they are either in the evangelical wing of the Christian right, or among the "new" evangelicals. To determine which requires one more set of questions.

- *Political Perspective Questions.* Interviewees who respond positively to social engagement questions should then be asked about party and ideology. If they strictly endorse the Republican Party and the staunchly conservative wing of the political spectrum, then they are likely part of the traditional evangelical wing of the Christian right. If not, if they are more independently oriented and endorse ideas and candidates from both parties, then they are likely part of the "new" evangelicals. As such, they are not part of the Christian right and likely to think and vote in a more principled centrist fashion.

In sum, it is best not to classify categorically any person or organization as simply being part of the Christian right. That could refer to a fundamentalist whose perspective may be fairly anti-social, or to a traditional evangelical who is politically sophisticated but subsumed by the Republican Party. It is best therefore to be more precise based on the interview sequence listed above. Even more importantly, it is critical not to lump the "new" evangelicals in with the Christian right, since the "new" evangelicals are more closely aligned with another group altogether—the principled centrists. For example, it is likely that "new" evangelicals' voting patterns will more closely resemble those of secular principled centrists than those of the Christian right. These are trends that journalists and researchers must understand clearly in order to accurately report on key blocks of religious Americans.

SUGGESTIONS FOR FURTHER READING

Avalon, John. 2004. *Independent Nation: How the Vital Center Is Changing American Politics.* New York: Harmony.

Danforth, John. 2006. *Faith and Politics: How the "Moral Values" Debate Divides America and How to Move Forward Together.* New York: Penguin Books.

Hunter, James Davison. 1991. *Culture Wars: The Struggle to Control the Family, Art, Education, Law, and Politics in America.* New York: Basic Books.

Kemeny, P. C., ed. 2007. *Church, State and Public Justice: Five Views.* Madison: InterVarsity Press.

Lindsay, D. Michael. 2007. *Faith in the Halls of Power: How Evangelicals Joined the American Elite.* New York: Oxford University Press.

Skillen, James W. 1994. *Recharging the American Experiment: Principled Pluralism for Genuine Civic Community.* Michigan: Baker Publishing Group.

Waldman, Steven. 2008. *Founding Faith: Providence, Politics, and the Birth of Religious Freedom in America.* New York: Random House.

DISCUSSION QUESTIONS

1. The author gives examples from the same newspaper, *The Washington Post*, of very different readings on religion and faith over a period of recent years. Why do you think this is so? Is it differences in the understanding and perspectives of the writers, or the evolution of the general understanding in the press about religion, or some combination of both? Explain.

2. In what sense does someone's faith inform his or her politics and why is this important for journalists to know?

3. Fundamentalists, evangelicals, and 'new' evangelicals (or neo-evangelicals) are often lumped together in the media as the Christian right. Explain how this is confusing and inaccurate citing the significant differences among these groups.

4. How does the concept of principled centrism apply in situations where voters do not march in lockstep with the old paradigm of liberal-Democrat or conservative-Republican? Give examples of how principled centrism applies in a style of politics and policymaking that is neither left nor right wing.

5. Discuss the author's sequence of questions near the end of the chapter for "drilling down" to understand people from the world of Christian faith when reporting and writing stories.

ENDNOTES

1. Michael Weisskopf, *Washington Post,* sec. A1, February 1, 1993.

2. E. J. Dionne, Jr., *Washington Post,* sec. A13, August 19, 2008.

3. Krista Tippett, *Speaking of Faith,* 2009, http://speakingoffaith.publicradio.org (accessed July 1, 2009).

4. Sally Quinn and John Meacham, *On Faith,* November 9, 2006, http:/newsweek.washingtonpost.com/onfaith (accessed July 1, 2009).

5. Office of the Press Secretary, *Obama Announces White House Office of Faith-Based and Neighborhood Partnerships,* February 5, 2009.

6. George Gallup, Jr., *The Gallup Poll: Public Opinion 2003,* November, 2004.

7. *Webster's New Collegiate Dictionary,* Merriam-Webster, 1979, s.v. "Religion."

8. Timothy Kelly, "The Role of Religion, Spirituality, and Faith-Based Community in Coping with Acts of Terrorism," in *Psychology of Terrorism,* ed. Bruce Bongar et al., New York: Oxford University Press, 2007.

9. In the past a third term was also used to describe members of the Christian right — "born-again Christians." This referred to those who claim a personal commitment to Jesus Christ that is important in their daily life, and believe they are heaven-bound

because they have confessed their sins and accepted Jesus Christ as their savior (The Barna Group 2008). However, fewer Christians currently self-identify as being "born again" (though they may agree with the tenets thereof) so the term is no longer widely used.

10. R. A. Torrey, ed., *The Fundamentals: A Testimony to the Truth,* 1988 (reprint).

11. E.g., Dr. Harold Ockenga who helped found Fuller Theological Seminary in Pasadena, CA, which today is the world's largest accredited seminary. Fuller is known for representing a 'new' evangelical Christian perspective—engaged with society and the social issues of the day—and not beholden to either side of the political spectrum.

12. David Bebbington, *Evangelicalism in Modern Britain: A History from the 1730s to the 1980s,* 1989.

13. Richard Neuhaus, *The Naked Public Square: Religion and Democracy in America,* 1986.

14. John Avlon, *Independent Nation,* 2004.

15. John Avalon, "What Independent Voters Want," *Wall Street Journal,* October 20, 2008: A19.

16. It is important to note that different pollsters define "Evangelical" differently, which is why the reported size of the Evangelical voting block varies from less than 10 percent to over 50 percent. The definition used in this article is simply based on those who self-describe as Evangelical.

17. The Barna Group, "How People of Faith Voted in the 2008 Presidential Election," *The Barna Group,* November 11, 2008. http://www.barna.org/barna-upgrade/article/13-culture/18-how-people-of-faith-voted-in-the-2008-presidential-race (accessed July 1, 2009).

18. Amy Sullivan, *Time/CNN,* November 5, 2008.

19. Comment made during Warren's annual AIDS conference, December, 2006.

20. The author of this chapter currently serves as the Institute's director. See www.depree.org.

21. Timothy Kelly, "Obama Must Govern from the Center," *Pasadena Star-News,* March 2, 2009: A14.

CHAPTER 12

Religious Pluralism: Getting to Know a Faith Tradition

Munir A. Shaikh

The author is executive director of the Institute on Religion and Civic Values, based in Fountain Valley, CA. Formerly the Council on Islamic Education, the institute has extensive experience working with publishers, educators, and scholars to redress stereotyping about Islam in books and other literature. The council developed standards to insure a proper understanding of any religious tradition. These are applicable to journalism, and can be extended to all faith-based perspectives that may be unfamiliar to reporters, editors, and bloggers.

The first World's Parliament of Religions, held in September 1893, in Chicago, signaled a readiness on the part of a small yet significant proportion of the American public to view religious pluralism in terms of "inclusion" rather than mere "toleration."[1]

The unprecedented nature of the gathering lent it a seminal quality and epochal status in broadening the majority culture's conception of diversity and shared public space.[2] Following in the footsteps of those marginalized on the basis of gender and race (i.e., those sidelined for other than religious reasons), Jews, Catholics, and other religious outsiders invoked the language of "inclusion" to claim their place within the "melting pot" metaphor that gained currency in the early twentieth century.[3]

As the United States became more industrialized, the variety of belief systems that confronted people in urban areas led to conversion to different Christian denominations, or even to another religion, as well as increased inter-religious unions. These shifts carried less of a stigma than in Europe.[4] While Christianity remained vital among African Americans, many became reacquainted with Islam as one of their ancestral West African religions. In the Cold War era, the civil rights movement paved the way for changes in the U.S. immigration quota policies. The Immigration Act of 1965 enabled millions of individuals from Asia and other regions to come to the United States. This signaled the emergence of a much more significant landscape of religious and cultural pluralism in America, in which assimilation to dominant Euro-American norms was no longer a foregone conclusion, and new conceptions of multiculturalism and integration emerged.

To help readers make sense of some dimensions of these profound shifts, the Religion Newswriters Association was established in 1949 by 12 religion beat journalists.[5] A foundation was established in 1999 to sustain the organization's efforts to help journalists cover religion with balance, accuracy, and insight, and improve the public's understanding of religion.[6] Its advice to journalists with the advent of the Internet is discussed in Chapter 5 by the organization's head, Debra Mason.

Journalists as Educators

The press, in its many incarnations, functions as an important bulwark of liberty. Journalists, by dint of their profession, tend to be on a never-ending quest in search of "the scoop," if not "the truth," in service to the public good. Yet the popular image of this work obscures what some might consider the more mundane—but no less important—role of reporting newsworthy stories of general interest on a day-to-day basis. In other words, the public education aspects of reporting are in line with Thomas Jefferson's belief that an active press is an essential means for educating the populace. This civic role for journalism, along with other institutional and discursive mechanisms, reinforces and over time reinscribes our self-image as Americans.

In this respect, journalists are at base educators. This assertion may give some news professionals pause, since academic freedom and press freedom exhibit key distinctions. However, the attempt to present an unfamiliar subject in a balanced, accurate, and insightful way remains a cornerstone in both frameworks. Indeed, "in open democratic societies, people view the press as a public forum for clarifying issues and problems, and perhaps to hear solutions."[7]

I want to make the case that what has happened already in the world of education has direct bearing on the world of journalism. These may seem like completely different worlds. However, there are strong parallels. This will involve a discussion first of the extraordinary developments in the area of increasing understanding of world religions in classrooms, textbooks and educational materials. I will go on to argue that much of what has been learned about how best to understand our new religious pluralism in the field of education can be very instructive for journalists who are presented with a vast array of information about traditions. Taking the time to understand these principles can prepare journalists for the times when they must make sense of complex stories either on deadline or in longer forms of reporting. To illustrate the principles, the coverage of Islam will be used as a case study in what follows. Other religious traditions can be addressed in analogous ways.

It is worthwhile to review some critical developments in the U.S. K–12 arena having to do with coverage of the world religions as part of history-science curricula. This is mainly within the context of world history and world cultures and geography instruction. The goal is to see if knowledge of such developments can enrich the efforts of journalists to inform their readers through stories involving religion.

Lessons from the 'Civic Public School'

Within the last two decades, three key factors have helped usher in the era of the "civic public school."[8] This is a term used today by observers to signify the commitment schools are making to educate students about others in our diverse religious and ethnic population based on constitutional, or First Amendment, principles.

First, the emergence of World History as a legitimate integrating field of academic scholarship and teaching has occasioned new approaches to the narrative of human societies and their interactions over time, supplanting the older "Western Civilization"-focused account. The role of religion in history is beginning to be told on a broad canvas, and religion is discussed more often as an integral rather than marginal factor in human affairs.

For example, the National Council for the Social Studies argues that studying about religion ought to be a key part of the social studies curriculum, and that to exclude it creates a wrongful impression about the role of religion in people's experience. It sees value in such study to prevent prejudice and contribute to understanding.[9]

Second, the development of consensus in the mid-1990s on the question of "religion in the schools" among major U.S. educational and religious organizations has begun to create a comfort zone for parents and educators with respect to addressing religion in a secular, academic setting. This consensus is reflected in publications such as the First Amendment Center's *A Teacher's Guide to Religion in the Public Schools,* containing answers to many questions about religion in the curriculum, accommodation of students' religious obligations, guest speakers on religion, observance of religious holidays, educators' religious beliefs, religious clubs, and related topics.[10]

There is broad agreement now among many educational and religious groups on the following: public schools may not inculcate nor inhibit religion; they must be places where religion and religious conviction are treated with fairness and respect; they uphold the First Amendment when they protect the religious liberty rights of students of all faiths and none; and they demonstrate fairness when they ensure that the curriculum includes study about religion, where appropriate, as an important part of a complete education. Teaching about religion means that the school's approach to religion is *academic,* not *devotional;* the school strives for student *awareness* of religions, but does not press for student *acceptance* of any religion; the school sponsors study *about* religion, not the *practice* of religion; the school may *expose* students to a diversity of religious views, but may not *impose* any particular view; the school *educates* about all religions; it does not *promote* or *denigrate* any religion; the school *informs* students about various beliefs; it does not seek to *conform* students to any particular belief.[11] The import of such consensus for enriching our national conversation about religion in schools and establishing a solid baseline for reasonable policymaking cannot be stressed enough.

Lastly, in the latter half of the 1990s, the push for national — and subsequently state-level — academic standards in history, social science, and geography led policy-makers and educators to call for the integration of knowledge about the world religions in the requirements for student learning. In other words, scholars and curriculum designers are directed to incorporate scholarship on religion as part of the effort to improve world history teaching.[12]

These three substantial development strands have established a trajectory for improved educational coverage, in terms of scope and accuracy, of those religions (Islam, Judaism, Hinduism, and Buddhism, as well as Native American, African, and other religious traditions) that previously received scant attention in U.S. K–12 textbooks and supplemental materials. Even the academic treatment of Christianity has seen dramatic improvement through a more nuanced historical presentation and inclusion of multiple faith perspectives that was typically lacking in prior decades.

Textbooks produced since the mid-1990s cover the major faiths' key figures, scriptures, teachings, and roles in shaping history and contemporary life. In the case of the coverage of Islam, images of deserts, camels, and heavily-veiled women have given way to a wide selection including Islamic craftwork and architecture, photographs of people in varied contemporary socio-economic and religious contexts, and engaging illustrations from medieval manuscripts.

The narratives of the rise of Islam, the development of Muslim civilization and its interactions with other cultures, the political dynasties, the role of trade, science, and the arts, and the changes experienced by Muslim societies in the face of European expansion and colonialism, have all seen more substantive and nuanced attention in multiple textbooks. Similar improvements can be seen in the coverage of various world civilizations, and attempts to present integrated history rather than covering cultures in isolation continue to increase.

U.S. publishers have welcomed scholarship-based information that strengthens their textbooks, and each generation of books tends to slowly, yet steadily, improve upon the last as authors avail themselves of new world history scholarship and pedagogical tools. Even so, problematic coverage reasserts itself periodically in the complex process of textbook production, indicating the need for further professional development for authors, editors, and educators related to teaching about religion. As of yet, though the scholarship is available to tell the story of the world in more interesting and equitable ways, an "institutional memory" to permanently sustain such an orientation in K–12 instructional materials has yet to take hold.

Since religion had been absent from most textbooks and curricular frameworks until relatively recently (a situation dubbed the "naked school," which was the polar opposite of the preceding "sacred school" era in which religious instruction took place alongside secular education), administrators and teachers have long been confused about the place of religion in schools. The "civic school" model now being propagated strikes a balance between indoctrination in religion on the one hand, and the exclusion of religion on the other.

The civic grounding emphasized today also enables school administrators to provide reasonable religious accommodation to students of diverse backgrounds without promoting any particular set of beliefs. Thus, students have been allowed to gather for prayer among themselves at appropriate moments outside of class time, request foods that meet religious dietary needs, and express their respective religious viewpoints. In the United States, religious attire worn by students has also been considered an expression of religious liberty rights, rather than a violation of church-state separation or the American conception of secularity. Education professionals increasingly are becoming familiar and comfortable with this model, enhancing the prospect of greater religious literacy among Americans in the coming years. Whereas the "sacred schools" and "naked schools" privileged or marginalized religion respectively, pleasing some while alienating others, the "civic school" can serve as a critical institution to enable U.S. citizens to learn to live with their deepest differences.

From Schools to Newsrooms

Let us now go on to the question of news coverage and what can be learned from the changing world of education. This overview on what's happened in schools is not simply a point of information about the state of pre-collegiate social studies. The trends in K–12 described above have their analogues in the news world and in the public square, arising from the same general societal impulses. A report in 2000 on "Religion in American Public Life" took note of increased religion coverage on television and the creation of "faith and values" sections in newspapers. It said, on the other hand,

> [r]eligious perspectives on science, technology, ethical questions, and the arts . . . rarely see the light of day in either print or broadcast media. In many cases, reporters find it hard to come to terms with the religious motivations of the people they write about.[13]

The report goes on to state that the journalistic tendency to sensationalize can be particularly distorting of religion, and that extreme religious views receive more attention than mainstream perspectives.[14] Of course, the burgeoning of religion news staffs in the late 1990s, as reflected in the comment above, had yet to contend with the new market realities produced by the Internet and new forms of media consumption which have caused a contraction in print coverage. While religion as such remains as important as ever as a topic of news coverage, the religion beat itself has undergone significant transformations.

It is therefore all the more important for a broad cadre of writers and editors to operate along the lines of common standards and principles. In addition to the grounding in journalistic ethics that one expects of news professionals, it behooves religion writers to consider principles of religion coverage that are shared by educators as they seek to buttress their training and navigate their relationship to the subjects of their stories.

Useful Guidelines for Journalists

The guidelines above regarding what schools may or may not do with regard to religious content and practice can carry over into public square conversations between members of different faiths as well as between them and those who hold no faith. To be clear, this is not to suggest that devotional attitudes or acts should not be manifested in our shared space, but that each of us ought to be conscious about our respective religious liberty rights and eschew denigration of any given faith or coercive efforts to conform individuals to a given set of beliefs. Insofar as journalists who encounter religion in their work are concerned, they must simply and consistently verify that their writings do not inadvertently privilege one religion over another, or one form of religious understanding over another. Rather than mere recourse to notions of "objectivity," "neutrality," or "detachment," taking the following broad criteria into consideration can help religion writers shape meaningful stories that reflect accurate yet sensitive coverage. They can be as beneficial to journalists as they are to educators.

Natural Inclusion: coverage of religion should take place within a historical or cultural context, covering only what is essential to understanding events or peoples. This may appear to be self-evident, but in many cases religious dimensions of a story are treated ahistorically. In particular, religion, rather than more mundane, worldly factors, is often seen as shaping culture and providing specific motivations for reported actions. For example, leading up to the 2008 presidential election, a number of op-ed articles and news stories engaged the question of whether Barack Obama was seen as a lapsed Muslim (i.e., an apostate) by American Muslim voters and Muslims abroad. This theological exercise, ironically conducted by non-Muslim commentators, did not in any way cohere with the actual attitudes and priorities of the voters being speculated about. In terms of covering adherents to Islam in the United States, in the national media the coverage of Muslims of immigrant origins tends to be much greater than that given African-American Muslims (who have a longer history as Americans, represent the largest ethnic grouping among Muslim-Americans, and are predominantly mainstream believers). The criteria of natural inclusion would suggest that this community be treated not as marginal or incidental in the story of American Islam, but rather as central. At the very least, this segment of the community should be well represented in a cosmopolitan presentation of Islam in America.

Fairness and Balance: writers should strive to ensure that no religious or anti-religious point of view is advocated, and critical thinking about historical or contemporary events involving religious traditions is advanced without engendering cynicism. The use of attributive language, second nature to experienced journalists and educators alike, is vital in order to avoid qualitative comparisons between religions and to compare and contrast different perspectives that religious groups might have on any number of issues. Statements need proper attribution to authoritative sources so that the writing does not wander into characterizations that seem like opinions. Avoid the use of adjectives such as "radical," "moderate," and "militant" without proper sourcing.

Respect for Differences: in assessing the place of one's own sensibilities or predispositions, it is important to take care not to present religious truth claims as relative or to reduce all religions to a common denominator. It is equally problematic to "explain away" religious faith as merely social or psychological phenomena, even though it is necessary to examine the social, economic, and cultural contexts in which religions have formed and changed. Descriptive language that reports how people of faith interpret their own practices and beliefs, and how these beliefs have affected people's lives historically and today, will go a long way toward accurately reporting differences in a way that preserves the respective normative views of various communities.

Use of Religious Scriptures: in the context of the classroom, classical religious texts may be included as part of the study of history and literature. Journalists, like educators, must do their best to cite passages along with the contexts in which they have been understood. While faith adherents often apply passages in ways that transcend place and time, writers should note that the universals emanate from historical particulars. On the matter of style and structure, it is critical not to measure one faith's scriptures by the conventions of that of another. For example, to describe a text as "confusing" or "without coherent narrative" is to do a disservice to religious traditions in which clearly the scriptures do make sense. Certainly, each of the world's sacred texts has its own qualities and characteristics, and is to be approached on its own terms. In reporting stories, it should be conveyed that there may be several differing interpretations of passages and texts within each religious tradition, and this is often the case surrounding debates about contentious social or political issues. In reporting how such texts are deployed by authority figures or others to advance specific viewpoints or positions, it is important to check the tendency to use labels such as "liberal," "traditional," "conservative," and the like. It is best to simply state the interpretations and allow readers to make their own inferences.

Applying the Guidelines to Coverage of Islam

The way efforts to improve knowledge about Islam have been carried out in the last few decades makes for a useful case study. Just as the content in social studies books from the 1970s and 1980s on the topic of the Middle East, Islam, or Muslim cultures frequently violated the above guidelines, so did many mainstream media articles on these topics. In a sense textbooks were simply a genre of texts that shared basic features with other types of texts available for public consumption. Indeed "one could compose an extensive rogues' gallery of errors in the description of Islam, its origins, beliefs, and practices"[15] that extended across a variety of Western cultural products. This may be simply because journalists proceed from what they think are familiar contexts to the public.[16] This is exacerbated by the fact that "public relations professionals, partisan sources, and other 'spin doctors' all attempt to define the story for news people, forcing the reporter to hone his or her critical faculties."[17]

Yet even critical thinking may have its limits, at least in terms of being subject to established paradigms of thought. Mark Silk, professor of Religion in Public Life at Trinity College, notes that traditional western religious values inform interpretations of events, and that "these values are embodied in a series of moral formulas, or topoi, that shape the way religion stories are conceived and written."[18] These topoi may be understood as "moral least common denominators" that invoke familiar meanings shaped by social context.[19] Silk identifies seven topoi guiding religion journalism: good works, tolerance, false prophecy, hypocrisy, inclusion, super-natural belief, and declension.[20] Most significantly, "the more widely shared (by the public) a view expressed in a news story, the less noticed the topoi will be."[21]

The phenomenon of Orientalism provides additional topoi with regard to coverage of newer American religious traditions that are demographically comprised of a significant immigrant or "new American" component. Hand in hand with the notion of a static, undynamic "East" has been the image of the dynamic, progressive West, undergirded by Enlightenment ideals and values. Indeed, in the public square, let alone policy circles, the meta-narrative of progress, modernity, development continues to be held up as the prism through which other nations and societies are evaluated and judged. A common theme, or topos, emerging from this vantage point is the notion that Islam is due for a Reformation along the lines of what occurred in European Christianity. By following in the footsteps of European nations, Muslim countries, and the rest of the developing world, might someday achieve liberty, equality, and fraternity. On the pages of newspapers, there is little room, when it comes to religion qua religion, for trenchant structural analysis of colonial legacies and world systems theories, to say nothing of post-modern intellectual turns that lay bare our cultural and political predispositions and commitments.

Consequently, lively scholarly debate regarding how best to understand the place of Islam and Muslim societies in the modern world largely remains relegated to the ivory tower, while popular discourses about Islam and Muslims remain fraught with crude stereotypes and misunderstanding. This is changing, of course, with improved education at the K–12 level as indicated above, as well as increasing civic engagement and community involvement on the part of Muslim-Americans. Even so, a fundamental and recurring problem is the conflation of Islam as a faith tradition and specific political ideologies that employ religious language to garner support for particular causes. This is a part of the overall problem of illiteracy regarding the faith among many Westerners. Moreover, the perceived interests reflected in Western states' political and economic policies in the Middle East region, and the role of the media in propagating accepted vantage points, have also shaped popular views and stereotypes. The trope of Western modernity and non-Western backwardness is well represented in Hollywood films and contemporary literature. News headlines often present sensational or exceptional events as somehow being motivated by Islamic religious teaching.

Shifts in the broad discursive issues broached above will require sustained efforts by many conscientious individuals operating in a variety of professional capacities, including educators, journalist, artists, faith leaders, and community activists, and such shifts will be shaped by America's evolving place on the world stage. However, change takes place incrementally and cumulatively. Revisiting our approach to some basic conceptual and terminological issues related to Islam can serve as a starting point for the envisioned evolution in coverage of the faith and its adherents.

It is encouraging to see that journalism stylebooks in use today, such as the AP Stylebook, include numerous terms pertaining to Islam and other faith traditions. Since there are a number of conventions in use for transliterating words in other languages such as Arabic and Persian into English and other European languages, it is important to select one and remain consistent. Among news professionals, long-standing spellings have remained in use, although academic specialists have evolved more precise transliteration systems with the use of special characters and markings. While this is impractical for journalists writing for a non-specialist audience, newsrooms should consider following the scholarly lead of such publications as the *International Journal for Middle East Studies*. Consequently, the term "Koran" would appear as "Qur'an", and so forth. In most cases, these renderings would be more welcome to faith adherents than older conventions. Translation is also important. Most notably, the term "Allah" should be translated as "God" rather than remain untranslated, except in direct quotes.[22]

Another significant issue involves the use of "Islamic" as an all-purpose adjective for anything pertaining to Islam or Muslims. Muslims themselves make distinctions regarding their core religious doctrines and practices that are well-rooted in the scripture or in the reported practice of the Prophet Muhammad, and their cultural attitudes, activities, and products. Of course, their faith informs many of these cultural norms and predispositions. The conscientious use of "Islamic" and "Muslim" as adjectives also serves to convey the distinction between the ideals embodied in the faith tradition and the realities experienced or expressed on the ground. It is recommended that the term "Islamic" be used infrequently, in reference to the more universal features of Islamic belief and practice, and the term "Muslim" be used as a de-facto adjective pertaining to the actions of Muslims. For example, it would be better to use "Muslim countries" or "Muslim-majority countries" rather than "Islamic countries."

Along these lines, it is imperative to resist the temptation to use the common "Muslim world" label to discuss the cultural and geographical aggregate of Islam. Such language reinforces "symbolic boundaries through the 'container' model of history, ring fencing narratives that are deemed to be alien and politically awkward."[23] It is much more meaningful and relevant to note the particular geographic region (i.e., Southwest Asia, North Africa, Southeast Asia, etc.), or actual countries (Egypt, Pakistan, Indonesia, etc.) being covered. Muslims are no more homogenous than Christians, but shared traits (which are by definition religious) could be discussed with reference to the word "ummah" (worldwide Muslim community).

Lastly, it is undeniable that most journalists have encountered the term "jihad." Perhaps most also know that this word literally means "struggle," "striving," and "exertion." In the context of Islamic teachings, jihad refers to "striving for the sake of God." Clearly, the word is employed in a variety of ways, including those involving combat or the use of violence for aims that are believed to be justified. In any event, jihad should not be translated as "holy war." This is a commonplace term that emanates from European Christian usage, but such a notion that "war" could be imbued with "holiness" is not attested in Islamic tradition. While righteous struggle is commendable, acts of terrorism were clearly labeled as *hirabah,* or "wanton violence," by Muslim jurists. In news coverage, journalists who are able to flesh out such dimensions of the rich thought in classical Islamic tradition, going beyond easy references to "Shari'a", would serve their readers well.

A number of other conceptual and terminological issues are addressed in resources now available to educators. Journalists are encouraged to seek these out to better equip themselves for addressing this challenging, sensitive subject.

Conclusion

At the most recent Parliament of the World's Religions, held on December 3–9, 2009, in Melbourne, Imam Abdul Malik Mujahid of Chicago was elected chair of the Board of Trustees of the council. This is just one indication of the changing landscape of religious life in the world. Awareness of religion has begun to replace wariness of religion, insofar as the recognition of religion's continuing relevance to understanding global events is concerned. Closer to home, paternalistic attitudes that saw diversity through the prism of cultural exoticism have begun to be replaced by a cosmopolitan sense of cultural pluralism as an intrinsic strength that will shape America's future.

The lessons learned in the U.S. education arena with regard to teaching about religions can assist journalists meet the challenge of reporting about religion in the news. Already, a great variety of news stories have moved beyond "primer" presentations of Islam and other faiths to explore the lived experiences of Muslims in various situations. By considering such guidelines, this tendency can only be strengthened. Muslims, and other religious groups, may now be found in their respective American contexts. The emerging human stories reinforce the fact that while many of these "new" religions may in fact not be so new, the new multireligious landscape is prompting journalists, like educators, to find new ways to talk about religious pluralism.

DISCUSSION QUESTIONS

1. How much of your own formal education involved learning about religions? In what ways does the author suggest that things have changed today?

2. What if anything did you learn in all the institutional settings of your life, either schools, churches, or workplaces, about religions other than your own?

3. Pick two traditions that you were not raised in and discuss what you know about them right now. How comfortable are you that this information is accurate and that your perceptions are correct?

4. What does the author mean when he suggests there are parallels between learning about religion in school and practicing good journalism today in a diverse nation?

5. Imagine you were asked to cover a controversy over the approval by planning authorities of a new mosque to be built in a suburban area. Apply the standards from this chapter and say how you would go about getting ready to do the reporting on this subject.

ENDNOTES

1. William R. Hutchison. *Religious Pluralism in America: The Contentious History of a Founding Ideal* (Yale University Press, 2003), 112.

2. Ibid.

3. Ibid, 113.

4. Religious Pluralism in the United States. The Boisi Center Papers on Religion in the United States (2007), 7.

5. *Reporting on Religion: A Primer on Journalism's Best Beat* (Religion Newswriters Association, 2006), 95.

6. Ibid.

7. John Dart, "Covering Conventional and Unconventional Religion: A Reporter's View," in *Review of Religious Research,* 39:2 (1997), 147.

8. Charles C. Haynes. "From Battleground to Common Ground: Religion in the Public Square of 21st Century America," in *Religion in American Public Life: Living with Our Deepest Differences* (W. W. Norton, 2001), 101.

9. Robert J. Dilzer. *Including the Study about Religions in the Social Studies Curriculum: A Position Statement and Guidelines* (Washington, DC: National Council for the Social Studies, 1984).

10. Charles C. Haynes. *A Teacher's Guide to Religion in the Public Schools.*

11. Haynes and Nord. *Finding Common Ground.*

12. In an assessment co-published with the First Amendment enter in 2000 called *Teaching About Religion in National and State Social Studies Standards,* our organization evaluated standards and program frameworks in seven national curriculum documents, most of which were published in the early 1990s, as well as the academic standards documents adopted or undergoing adoption by most of the 50 states in the late 1990s. We found that despite variations in the state standards, the recognition of the importance of religion within the history-social science curricula was indeed attested in virtually every state. However, the report also warns that the presence of religion in the standards will not necessarily translate into serious academic treatment of religion in the curriculum. The report makes a number of recommendations for reform, such as improving treatment of religion in textbooks, including knowledge about religion as test items in assessment, and offering in-service and pre-service educational opportunities for teachers in religious studies.

13. "Religion in American Public Life," 96th American Assembly, March 23–26, Harriman, NY, 168.

14. Ibid.

15. Susan L. Douglass, "Teaching about Religion, Islam, and the World in Public and Private School Curricula," in *Educating the Muslims of America* (Oxford University Press, 2009), 87.

16. Dart, 148.

17. Dart, 145.

18. Cited in Dart, 145. Mark Silk. *Unsecular Media: Making News of Religion in America.* Urbana, IL: University of Illinois.

19. Ibid.

20. Ibid.

21. Ibid, 146.

22. Editor's note: ReligionWriters.com has an online ReligionStylebook, which has been adopted throughout this book. To see how style is handled there for any number of entries, consult http://www.religionwriters.com/tools-resources/religionstylebook.

23. Shiraz Thobani, "Peripheral vision in the national curriculum: Muslim history in the British educational context," in Gerdien Jonker and Shiraz Thobani, eds. *Narrating Islam: Interpretations of the Muslim World in European Texts* (London: Tauris Academic Studies, 2010), 248.